PRAISE FOR *STEP UP*

"A useful, easy-to-digest road map for leading with clarity, compassion, and transparent communication. *Step Up* gives both tenured and new leaders fresh ideas and creative reminders that will propel them to new heights as they motivate and inspire those around them to meet and exceed their goals."
- **Melissa Reiff**, president and chief operating officer, The Container Store

"As Evans and Foster so wisely point out in *Step Up*, most often leadership is in the moment. Drawing on their considerable experience, Evans and Foster identify six critical opportunities to lead, and they offer practical and tangible ideas about how anyone can 'step up' and take ownership of these moments. This book artfully unravels many of the complexities and demystifies the actions needed to make something positive happen. *Step Up* is a valuable addition to the library of all the leaders who want to make their teams and organizations more effective."
- **Jim Kouzes and Barry Posner**, authors, *The Leadership Challenge*

"Evans and Foster provide a catalyst for reflection as well as resources and tools for practice. I look forward to sharing *Step Up* with the leaders I work with as an internal executive coach. I know this will make a difference for them and the teams they lead."
- **Bob Andrews**, director, executive coaching, Gap Inc.

"Evans and Foster are strategy and leadership team experts. In *Step Up* they share a secret weapon for developing and retaining top talent: six moments that develop leadership at all levels of an organization. I don't do theory. *Step Up* is easy to understand and apply for generating better business results."
- **Nic Vu**, senior vice president, retail, adidas® Group

"Evans and Foster's six moments offer a fresh perspective and caused me to think differently about the leadership challenges I face. I will use and recommend *Step Up*."
- **Matthew E. Winter**, president, Allstate Personal Lines

"At the FBI, we realized that the most successful agents consistently demonstrated specific behaviors for building trust and credibility in the field. Evans and Foster do a great job of explaining the skills and competencies required for successful leadership. This is an easy-to-follow guide for generating leadership in both public and private sector organizations."
—Supervisory Special Agent Tim Turner (retired), FBI Academy, and associate professor, Anderson University and Columbia Southern University

"Evans and Foster point out that leadership is something we all do, even if we didn't understand our role as leaders before. With examples from widely known leaders and case studies from their consulting practice, *Step Up* shows how to manage and listen to our anger and anxiety, improving our mental models and creating emotional safety around us. This lively, accurate, and practical book will inspire readers."
—John D. Mayer, professor of psychology, University of New Hampshire, and author, *Personal Intelligence*

"If you think that emotional intelligence is about being nice or avoiding conflict and you see yourself as a leader, you'd better get this book. *Step Up* introduces you to the nitty-gritty of emotionally intelligent leadership. You'll find examples and suggestions on how to handle negative emotions and arm yourself for those make-or-break leadership moments."
—Steven J. Stein, author, *Emotional Intelligence for Dummies*

"Innovation requires decisiveness and tough discussions where assumptions and ideas are explored and challenged. In *Step Up*, Evans and Foster give a road map to help any organization gain a competitive edge by igniting leadership at every level of the organization."
—Soren Kaplan, author, *Wall Street Journal* best seller *Leapfrogging*

STEP UP

LEAD IN SIX MOMENTS THAT MATTER

Henry Evans and Colm Foster

FOREWORD BY MARSHALL GOLDSMITH

Published by Dynamic Results

3245 Main Street, Suite 235, #216, Frisco, TX 75034 - www.dynamicresults.com

Library of Congress Cataloging-in-Publication Data
Evans, Henry J.
Step up : lead in six moments that matter / Henry Evans and Colm Foster ; foreword by Marshall Goldsmith. - First edition.

pages cm
Includes bibliographical references and index.
ISBN 978-0-578-34160-6 (paperback)

1. Leadership. I. Foster, Colm. II. Title.
HD57.7.E93 2014
658.4'092—dc23
2014002422

Printed in the United States of America
FIRST EDITION
HB Printing 10 9 8 7 6 5 4 3 2 1

Contents

We dedicate this book to the people who step up and demonstrate leadership in important moments, with or without the official title and authority to do so.

Foreword

I've enjoyed working with Henry Evans in both university and corporate environments. I also appreciate and respect the research and approach of Dr. Colm Foster's work. They are an international team, and I know from working within some of the same client organizations that they bring high cross-cultural sensitivity and awareness to their work.

In my book *What Got You Here Won't Get You There*, I emphasized the need for people to recognize their need for change and to change when necessary. As a business author, I know that we have a difficult task when trying to serve the business community through our writing: to make the complex simple for busy people who don't have a lot of time to read what we are writing.

In this book, *Step Up*, Henry and Colm manage the difficult task of making the complex simple. They give the reader a clear understanding of six critical moments that matter and when leadership is required. Leadership is not an esoteric concept, and Henry and Colm do a great job of illustrating how anyone can lead, regardless of his or her title, and no matter where he or she may sit on the organization chart, so long as he or she recognizes opportunity and knows what to do when opportunity knocks.

Henry and Colm help bridge the gap between the needs of an organization and the needs of the human beings who sit within the organization. They are both former competitive martial artists, so they bring a certain balance of pragmatism, only doing what works, along with an intuitive sense of what people need. I hope you will find, as I did, that they present this balance in a simple and accessible series of behaviors that we can all demonstrate when there is a leadership void in the room. They bring a style that is both compassionate and practical.

Enough about them; let's talk about us, readers. Henry and Colm are challenging us to recognize special moments in which we can demonstrate leadership and then step up in those moments so that we can elevate the performance and social experience that people have working in organizations. This is a high calling. From my perspective, Henry and Colm are challenging us to be catalysts for positive change in the form of better business results and better relationships at work, through our own decisions, actions, awareness, and behaviors.

We've got the road map in this book. Now we need to get to work and start recognizing the moments that matter so that we can lead when they arise.

Marshall Goldsmith
Million-selling author of the *New York Times* bestsellers
MOJO and *What Got You Here Won't Get You There*

Introduction

In this book, we are going to share six critical leadership moments and what the highest-performing people—whatever their title—do when they are in one of those moments. Stepping up to exercise leadership in those moments will make the biggest difference to you in your own leadership journey.

The Six Moments

A leadership moment is an instance when you must make a choice. Will you intervene, or will you let the chance pass you by? Will you step up in those moments that might seem small but that significantly impact business results and relationships? They are the moments that the clients of our consulting practice repeatedly tell us present the biggest problems for them:

1. *Using anger intelligently in the workplace*. In Chapter One, we show you how to use anger to drive better business results while also building relationships and how to match the mood of a group to the tasks it needs to accomplish.
2. *Recognizing and dealing with "terminal politeness."* You and others may be avoiding important conversations that you should have. The focus of Chapter Two is to attack the idea, not the person.

3. *Making decisions when no one else is making them.* Chapter Three is about making and communicating clear decisions when they are difficult to make or when outcomes are uncertain. This chapter is about embracing a willingness to be wrong in order to drive action.
4. *Taking ownership when others are externalizing a problem.* In Chapter Four, we focus on discovering what your contribution to undesired project and relationship outcomes may be. We help you uncover the inherent biases that may lead you to be part of the problem.
5. *Identifying and leveraging pessimism.* Chapter Five is about understanding, appreciating, managing, and leveraging the pessimists in your organization. It is also about understanding and leveraging your own pessimism.
6. *Inspiring others to take action.* Chapter Six is about recognizing when you and others are stuck in unproductive and redundant dialogue. We show you how to reverse the momentum of these interactions so that you and others begin to focus on a solution or just "move on."

We will outline the research that explains each moment so that you can understand the organizational dynamics at work, and provide you with specific, practical ideas about how to plan for and seize the opportunities that these moments present. By adopting the ideas and tools in this book, you will be able to "step up" in leadership moments as they present themselves. Through practice and reflection, you will increase your skill in predicting when these opportunities will arise and improve your ability to exercise your leadership.

We have provided you with an easy-to-use fifteen-minute online Step Up Leadership Assessment. Please scan the QR code in the box to take the assessment, which will give you instant feedback on your leadership readiness and point you to the relevant chapters in this book that are most important for you.

The Book's Structure

Each of the first six chapters in the book describes a different moment and is divided into four sections:

- Our Promise, which describes what you can expect to learn in the chapter
- Recognize the Moment, which will help you spot the leadership moments and understand what is happening
- Step Up, which contains suggestions for how you can exercise leadership in the six moments that matter
- A summary of the main points in the chapter

Each chapter also includes a Step Up hyperlink (in the form of a QR code) that will connect you with additional online resources related to the chapter.

The Conclusion shows you how to take on the necessary role of Director of Emotional Safety and how to avoid being the most powerful but also the most dangerous person in your organization.

Please note that the examples used in the book are all drawn from our own direct experience, but the names and contexts have been changed to preserve the confidentiality of our clients.

The Process

Learning a skill is very different from studying for a test or learning how to program a spreadsheet; it is experiential. That kind of learning primarily involves practice; to change your behavior, you must actively engage in that new behavior for a significant period of time. Experiential learning theory generally identifies four main components:

- *Concrete experimentation.* You have to actually try new behaviors, not just think about them. In leadership, it is your action, not your intention, that matters. You have to practice specific behaviors, such as the ones we will show you in each chapter of this book.
- *Feedback.* You must get quality feedback from at least one partner—ideally, a skilled coach, but a trusted colleague will do.
- *Reflection.* You must deeply reflect on the results of your new behavior in an honest and compassionate way, by asking, "What was I trying to do?" "Who was I being in that moment?" and "How did that work out for me?"
- *Assimilation.* You need to understand and make sense of the behavior and the result in a way that sets up the next experiment, asking, "What am I going to do differently next time?" or "What action will I take based on what I learned?"

Many of our clients react to the idea of self-reflection by claiming that they are too busy. When most people think of reflection as part of their learning process, they imagine spending long periods of time, usually in silence and often in the lotus position. However, we have a much more pragmatic idea in mind, based on a concept we borrowed from our research with the Jesuit Order. Although we don't ask you to subscribe to any particular worldview, we simply hope that you're willing to accept leadership learning and insight from many and diverse sources.

The Jesuits talk about being a *contemplative in action*. They engage in a few minutes of reflection two to three times a day, during which they decide how they'll approach the challenges facing them that day. They pay special attention to situations in which they have not performed at their best, which seem to present themselves as habitual tendencies.

We ask that you simply find a self-reflection practice that works for you. It might involve writing in a reflective diary each day, using a particular intersection or train stop on the way to or from work as a trigger to spend several minutes in reflective time, or associating reflection with the first or last coffee of the day. You can also reflect by talking to another person. Whatever practice you choose, keep it short, sharp, and focused on what you were trying to do, what happened, and what you are going to do differently the next time. The key is to adopt psychologist Ellen Langer's rules for mindful reflection: attend to what is happening in the moment, forget about broad generalizations, suspend judgment (especially negative judgment), and cultivate "creative uncertainty."[1]

It is also useful to link the reflection time to some form of reward. One of our clients bought a particularly stylish pen that he used only for writing in his reflective diary, so he really looked forward to that exercise. Another did her reflection during her favorite part of her day, her daily walk between her office and a coffee shop, so that it became a habit that she looked forward to rather than a chore that she would eventually drop. The key is for the period of reflection to be short, focused on what you will do differently the next time, and regular. By integrating this practice into your day-to-day routine, you won't perceive it as yet another item on your to-do list.

Experience itself is not what matters so much as your ability and willingness to learn from your experience. This requires that you honestly reflect on that experience. Be kind to yourself as you consider how well you have performed in any given situation and as you more generally assess your capabilities and performance.

The six moments do not follow a strict sequence or pattern. You are free to dip in and out of the book and to focus on one particular aspect. Your ability to create change in one of these moments will actually cause positive effects in the others. You will gain maximum benefit if you can work on each of the moments consistently over a significant period of time. The scarcity of great leaders is not because the recipe is so complicated that few people can understand it; quite the opposite is true. It's that great leadership takes time, effort, perseverance, and a very high capacity to accept being wrong. By using the tools in this book, you will begin to see what is happening in a room full of people that you were not able to see before. You will cease being a bystander and become an active participant who can catalyze change in the moments that matter.

Our Experience

Over the last ten years, we have been fortunate enough to have earned and maintained the trust of thousands of executives and people throughout all levels of organizations around the world. We have been their thought partners in making critical decisions that affect the future of their individual careers, their personal lives, and their organizations. This sacred trust has afforded us a very special opportunity to observe the people who have earned the best reputations and reaped the best rewards and the behaviors those people consistently demonstrate.

We consider leadership to be an activity in which you engage rather than a position into which you are promoted or elected. It does not derive from your title or place on an organization chart. So although we work with people in leadership roles—and draw many of the book's examples from our interactions with them—you do not have to be in a role like this to exercise the kind of leadership we describe.

For example, while consulting for a biotech company, we worked with a midlevel manager, whom we will call Mary, along with her peers and her boss, a VP. The team was resource constrained and had aggressive targets set by the president of the company. When the VP came back to his team to report that a request for additional resources was turned down by the president, the emotional state of the team bottomed out. Most people felt frustrated and helpless. Mary recognized that the team was simply accepting this defeat, and she spoke up in an emotionally intelligent and somewhat controversial way, asking, "I know I'm the newest member of the team and that I might be missing a lot of information. I also know that the team I worked with in my last job would not have accepted this news after only one rejection."

Then, addressing the VP directly, Mary said, "I'm sure you did your best job of requesting more resources on our behalf. I'm wondering if we could spend some time as a team examining how you did that and see if we can find a different approach. If we don't try, we will be working overtime for months, and I will be wondering what we could have tried to create a win."

The VP welcomed the discussion, the team agreed on a new "ask," and, armed with a new approach, the VP tried again, ultimately getting most of what they asked for.

History has given us many examples of leadership emerging from unexpected places and from surprising people. Sometimes the leadership is demonstrated by people with no formal position of authority and in a quite passive way. Mahatma Gandhi and Martin Luther King Jr. are examples. Others used a more forceful approach, through military intervention or other forms of action, leveraging their authority to get great things out of people. For example, President Kennedy challenged the United States to put a man on the moon in ten years and return him safely to the earth.

Whatever your role, your colleagues come to you for your expertise. The person who labels and ships boxes on the warehouse floor of a distribution company might be at the bottom of the organization chart. But when a call comes in complaining that a shipment has not arrived, the expert on whether or not the product had actually been packed and shipped is that warehouse employee. And when he is responding, he has the potential to exercise leadership.

We start our leadership development programs by asking the participants whether they consider themselves to be leaders. No matter where in the world we are or the level of the executives and managers with whom we are working, the result is the same: hardly anyone in the room considers himself or herself to be a leader. When we ask people to nominate examples of good leadership, we get a list of the usual suspects from politics, business, and sports: Nelson Mandela, Aung San Suu Kyi, Steve Jobs, Richard Branson, and so on. We call these individuals leaders with a capital *L*. When people compare themselves to heroic leaders like these, it stops them from stepping up in leadership situations. They worry that they are not leaders because they lack experience or confidence, or don't have a big team of direct reports. They tell themselves that they will be a leader once they get the big promotion or the fancy title. True, they might not be as visionary as a Steve Jobs or as charismatic as a Nelson Mandela, but fretting over that is like refusing to enjoy swimming in your own pool because you will never make an Olympic final. We offer you a different model, one that you can use every day to optimize your leadership. It will allow you to gain the confidence and skill to grasp opportunities to exercise leadership when they arise. We strongly believe that everyone has leadership potential or, more precisely, the potential to exercise leadership in certain situations. There is a surprisingly small difference between the great leaders with whom we work and those who don't fully realize their potential: the great ones simply recognize and take advantage of leadership moments.

We also don't believe the claim that "anyone can be a great leader." This is akin to saying that anyone can be a World Cup–caliber soccer player. Leadership (with a capital *L*) requires a special set of skills, just as being a great athlete does. But anyone can recognize moments where leadership is required and know what to do once she realizes that she is in one of those moments. We appreciate what Jim Kouzes and Larry Posner wrote in their book *The Leadership Challenge*: "Teams, organizations, and communities need people to step up and take charge."[2]

The ideas in this book are deliberately cognitively simple. When our clients get feedback, they often ask us, "Is that it?" They expect a more intellectually challenging piece of information. As coaches and leadership development consultants, we have to resist the urge to add complexity to our ideas merely to satisfy a client's need to be intellectually challenged by the process. However, though our ideas may be simple to understand, it takes real effort to put them into practice consistently.

In short, common sense is not always common in practice.

You have the potential to be a true leader in your organization. All it takes are the ideas we offer you and the discipline and desire to step up consistently during these six moments. This book will help you understand the moments and the associated behaviors in which you can engage in real leadership. You will also have a clear picture of the behaviors to look for in others, which will allow you to decide on whom to promote, demote, hire, and fire, as well as whom to work for and work with.

CHAPTER ONE

Get Angry, Not Stupid

Anyone can become angry—that is easy. But to be angry with the right person, to the right degree, at the right time, for the right purpose, and in the right way—that is not easy.
—Aristotle

Our Promise

This chapter will show you how to use negative emotions such as anger to drive healthy and productive outcomes. Much of what you've learned about emotional intelligence is wrong. It's been taught incorrectly over the last thirty years, and emotional intelligence "experts" (ourselves included) have been part of the problem. This teaching has been based on the misconception that negative emotions are bad, interfere with rational thinking, and should be avoided or suppressed. Our goal in this chapter is to correct that misconception.

Everyone has heard that people should suppress or even completely avoid feelings such as anger and frustration in the workplace. However, we have observed our clients achieve outstanding business results doing what may seem counterintuitive.

We will show you how to be authentically angry or frustrated and to do it without leaving dead bodies in your wake or being labeled a jerk. Used intelligently, these feelings can actually build relationships.

We will also show you how to help others leverage negative emotion and how to help a group find the mood most appropriate for tackling the task in front of it.

Recognize the Moment

A team that led the regional division of a global company was responsible for hitting an annual forecast budget. In the middle of one particular year, the global office removed significant resources but left objectives unchanged, sending the message, "You still have to accomplish all these goals with only 70 percent of the resources promised. Don't whine about it. Get the job done."

There was a lot of anger and discussion about the unfairness of the global office's action. In a situation like this, fraught with negative emotion, we hope to see somebody on the team recognize a leadership moment and say, "You know what, folks? The reality now is that we have 70 percent of the budget we were promised, and it is OK to be angry. I'm angry, too. Now—how are we going to turn this anger around and use all this energy to achieve our very aggressive goal with 30 percent less budget?"

Think back and identify a time when you've felt angry at being unfairly treated. How did you and your colleagues react?

Taking advantage of such a moment requires two things:

- The awareness of one's own negative emotions and the ability to make productive use of them
- The skill to help others do the same

Thinking and Feeling

We used to make it our goal to drive bad moods and negative emotions *out* of organizations. Our old approach would have been to try to suppress or ignore that team's anger. We did the same in our own professional and personal lives, because we mistakenly believed that this was the right thing to do.

We have since changed our stance. We now know that people can leverage their "afflictive emotions"—those that make them feel bad, such as anger, greed, hate, guilt, or longing—to drive outstanding results. Nowadays, we have a better idea of how people's emotions influence what and how they think. We live in an age that places a high value on thinking. We all are often told, especially in Western societies, to avoid being "carried away" by our emotions, advice based on the flawed presumption that emotions interfere with rational thinking.

Few of us truly understand the link between how we are feeling and what we are thinking. Most of us operate on the principle that thinking would be better, clearer, and more efficient if we kept our feelings out of it. However, as neuroscientists have been saying for years, and management scientists are now beginning to realize, our thinking is completely bound up with our feelings. In fact, rather than seeing ourselves as thinking machines that have feelings, it would be more accurate to say that we are feeling machines that are capable of thought.

Think about a time when you purchased something that you knew was overpriced or that you could not really afford, only to regret it later. This is a clear example of how we sometimes feel first and think second.

These two understandings—that we can leverage afflictive emotions and that thinking and feeling are bound together—have important consequences for certain moments in which you might exercise leadership, moments such as the one described in the tale of the leadership team whose resources were suddenly cut.

The Anatomy of Anger

Anger is a good example of an afflictive emotion that is highly leverageable. Consider anger as a fuel that you can use to generate the energy required to move to productive action. Although a lot has been written about the power of positive emotion, all emotions—both positive and negative—have uses. Positive emotions are clearly more pleasurable, but that should not blind you to the fact that you can leverage your negative emotions to produce positive outcomes.

We had a client who was using anger unproductively to deal with her boss. Our client, the president of an industry-leading software division of a larger company, worked for a CEO whom she admired and also struggled with. She complained that he would go "skip level" and give direction to her employees, sometimes in a way that she felt contradicted a prior agreement. Another issue was that she felt as though she had to answer to an intermediary between her and the CEO, and that this individual was operating with a different belief system from her own and who simply did not add value. Her anger robbed her of the enjoyment she should have taken from her work and distracted her from bringing her full potential to bear on the challenges she faced.

Our client let her frustration over one or both of these perceived obstacles build up over time. Although she exceeded all metric-driven goals, she would sometimes "blow up" in meetings with the CEO and speak in a way that he found to be unproductive and annoying.

While coaching her, we helped her identify that both of her perceived frustrations had a connecting theme. She felt frustrated at being micromanaged or didn't have adequate autonomy for her role (or both). We helped her figure out that she needed to have a higher-level discussion with the CEO that centered on discussing how much autonomy she should have. She avoided discussing the intermediary's perceived incompetence or her CEO's skip-level tendencies. Instead of using her anger to complain, she started to use it to challenge the paradigm and to ask for a level of autonomy and respect that was commensurate with her role.

She was ultimately successful on both fronts. Her approach to the CEO was to say, "I'm interested in finding out if, as president of this division, I have the autonomy to make a financial decision of this size—even if it isn't what you would do if you were president of my division."

She managed to carefully redirect her energy, using it as fuel to deal with these redundant annoyances on a higher level.

Colm learned this lesson as a young martial artist—a national champion at underage level. Yet there was one fighter whom Colm had never beaten—the senior champion. In the gym at the back of Colm's house, he hung an article about the senior champion. Whenever he felt like quitting on the last set of reps, he focused on the picture of his rival, and the anger surge he felt gave him the fuel to push through. Anger may be a dangerous emotion to feel during a contest, but it is a very good emotion to feel during training.

A client of ours has used this technique to enhance the quality assurance level of his company's proposals. They had recently lost a competitive bid to a rival that had previously been below their capability—both on financial and technical criteria. The prospect's rejection letter incited a great deal of anger and soul searching in our client's leadership team. The leader skillfully used the anger that this rejection caused to focus attention on what the team would do to never let that happen again. When they're confident that they have produced a great bid on a new proposal, the leader reminds them of how angry they were when they lost to their new rival. He uses this anger to challenge them and inspire them to take their work to the next level. Just as in Colm's case, anger is not a good emotion to carry into a bid meeting, but it certainly helps during the long, dark nights of preparation leading up to that moment.

We see another great example of this in the case of Reddit, a web search company that was sold to Condé Nast eighteen months after it was founded. Although this seems like a fairy tale "rags to riches" story for the founders (University of Virginia students Alexis Ohanian and Steve Huffman), there were some real setbacks. One in particular shows how anger can be a useful fuel for business success.

While trying to get their project off the ground, Ohanian and Huffman were called to meet a Yahoo executive who was interested in their project. When the Yahoo executive heard that Reddit had only a few thousand users, he scoffed, "You're a rounding error compared to Yahoo."

Ohanian returned home and wrote, on the wall beside his desk, "You are a rounding error." Ohanian used that comment to recall the anger he felt at being dismissed, causing two things to happen. First, he was convinced that he was not a rounding error and that his business model was sound. His anger made him sure that he was right. Second, he used the energy his anger gave him to set out to prove the Yahoo guy wrong. Ohanian said, "That simple sentence of rejection fueled us."[1]

Think about a time when you have suffered a setback or a rejection of some kind. Rejection can be one of the hardest emotions to contend with. Did you dwell on the anger and humiliation? Did you plot all sorts of horrible acts of revenge against the person who rejected your idea or who you thought caused your failure? Did you waste precious time cursing your fate? Imagine how much better it would have been if you had channeled that anger into productive uses like those we've described here.

If you don't have a colleague who can help you leverage the energy of a bad mood or bad memory to be productive, you can use certain techniques on your own. We will show you some of those later in this chapter, but to use these tools most effectively, you need to understand what is going on inside you as anger builds.

We recognize that the distinctions among the three layers of the brain have received much attention in other books. However, because these distinctions are crucial to understanding how to use anger productively, we'll outline them here. The brain consists of these layers:

- The **reptilian brain** deals with the very basic functions, such as eating and sleeping.
- The **limbic system and hippocampus** handle the processing of emotions and the formation of memory, which are inextricably linked. Within the limbic system is a gland called the amygdala that watches for danger.
- The **neocortex** handles all of the sophisticated processing, such as that required for abstract thought, language, and mathematics. Signals are passed from your limbic system to your neocortex, where you "make sense" of the information you receive from your environment. So all the thoughts you have are colored by your emotions, and the way you feel at any point has a direct influence on the thoughts you generate.

As a result of this structure, your emotional system can sometimes take precedence over your thinking system.[2] We can all point to instances where perfectly obvious and rational decisions were ignored based on how people felt. You can

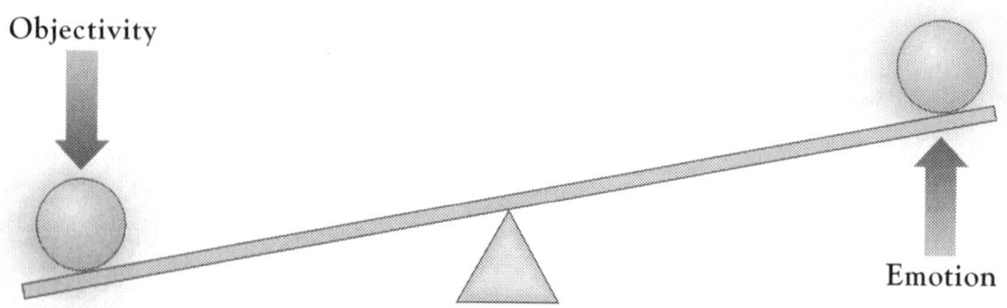

Figure 1.1 The Seesaw of Emotion vs. Objectivity
Copyright © Dynamic Results, LLC

probably recall a time when you felt so angry that you couldn't speak. Your amygdala was exciting a fight response, draining energy from your language center.

The problem for most people is not that they get angry; it's that they *become less intelligent* when they do. Our beef is with stupidity, not anger. So we don't want you to stop getting angry, as that would rob you of emotional fuel that you sometimes need to succeed. We simply want you to be *intelligent while angry*.

Figure 1.1 graphically represents how poorly managed emotion causes people to lose the ability to think objectively.

Be Angry with the Right Person

The quotation from Aristotle at the start of this chapter advises us of the importance of being angry with the right person. One predominant way that people deal with their anger is by taking that anger out on someone other than the source of their anger.

We worked with one very controlling senior executive who felt a need to manage every aspect of her environment, including her people and her strategy. She was dealing with a difficult stakeholder issue and was frustrated that one important group was refusing to engage in a productive way. However, the power dynamics of the situation prevented her from expressing her anger to those people, and she'd not yet learned to deal with her anger effectively.

She found herself becoming increasingly impatient and intolerant of her staff's mistakes. Once she developed more self-awareness and recognized her need for control, she was able to identify and accept how angry the reluctant stakeholder was making her. She then realized that she was carrying that anger around with her all the time—a low-grade mood of irritation that was merely anger waiting to be released. Sure enough, she would react in an impatient and frustrated way when one of her staff made a mistake. She experienced her breakthrough moment when she connected her impatience with her employee to her unresolved anger with the stakeholder who would not engage.

This client now recognizes that impatience with a staffer's mistake may signal a pivotal moment for her. She uses this simple awareness to handle her reactions. Now, when she feels as though someone isn't "coming through" for her, she understands that she is capable of thinking intelligently and brings herself in check prior to opening her mouth and actually speaking.

Take a moment now to think about people or situations in your work life that habitually cause you to become angry (or irritated or frustrated). Try to ignore the feelings you have toward the situation and ask yourself what it is that you are really angry about. Explore the possibility that the person or situation that is making you angry is a lightning rod for a real cause somewhere else in your life. What might that real cause be?

Step Up

The key to developing your ability to remain intelligent, even as your blood begins to boil, is to recognize that anger is not a binary, "either-or" emotion. That is, there are many levels of anger. At the mildest, you are slightly irritated, and then you become frustrated. If the situation persists, you become angry; and if the emotion continues to build, you may become enraged. To learn to remain intelligent while angry, you must start small—that is, learn to retain your thinking ability when you are merely irritated and then move on to frustration and so on.

Respond . . . Don't React

Our goal is to have you *respond* rather than *react*. A reaction is a somewhat thoughtless and sudden event, usually involving you saying or doing something you will later regret. A response comprises the behaviors and actions you thoughtfully planned to demonstrate when and if you were ever in a particular situation. Although there are rare situations when it is appropriate and perhaps even helpful to demonstrate negative emotion, we will first look at how to control your impulses during common and only mildly threatening situations.

The first step is to identify your "triggers": the types of people and situations that lead you into a highly charged emotional state. Some people get angry when they believe they are being lied to. Some have a negative emotional response when they perceive an injustice, such as racial discrimination or a large person picking on a smaller person. The members of the team whose budget was cut believed that they were being treated unfairly. The executive who was feeling as if her team wasn't coming through for her was misplacing her anger at her inability to control her situation. Those are the kinds of situations that decrease your intellectual and rational capacity. When was the last time you acted in anger and said (or did) something that you later regretted? Think about that situation now. Doing so will help you identify your triggers.

Ask yourself right now:

- *What type of* behavior *in others tends to make me feel upset?* Maybe a coworker who is always late on projects and always makes excuses bothers you. Or perhaps you're frustrated by people who "don't come through" or "lack accountability."
- *What types of* situations *tend to make me feel upset?* If you tend to get upset when stuck in traffic or when you have a delayed flight, you may be frustrated or angry when you can't control a situation.

After you have identified your personal triggers, you are equipped to do something about the anger that results. (Later we'll talk about the specific tactics you can use to manage your emotions.) For example, one of Henry's triggers is being lied to. The old Henry would feel anger and speak from that anger in a way that he would later regret. If you ever hear Henry give a keynote address, you are likely to hear him openly discuss mistakes he made while feeling very angry.

Perhaps you've had these moments too, when you say something that makes you feel better in the moment, but, in hindsight, leads you to think, "I could have done better than that." The new and improved Henry still feels angry when he perceives that he is being lied to. However, with good coaching, mentoring, practice, and study, he has developed methods for responding in a way that he can be proud of. Please note that although he has done a lot of introspective work to build the New Henry, Old Henry is alive and well and living in a bungalow in New Henry's backyard. When the weather isn't to Old Henry's liking, he comes out of the bungalow banging a pot and demanding immediate recognition.

Once you recognize that you are genuinely irritated with a person or situation yet can still be processing intellectually at a high level, you can move on to situations in which you experience frustration, then anger, and rage. Negative emotions can be very useful to you if you know how to manage them. However, they can be quite destructive if used unwisely—so we urge you to be careful and thoughtful about how and when you leverage these feelings.

Leaping to Judgment

You no doubt occasionally endure negative emotions when you are interacting with people whose beliefs differ from yours. While coaching, we often hear clients refer to someone else as "stupid." We ask that when faced with a divergent opinion, you don't judge the *entire human being* you're interacting with as ignorant, stupid, or evil. We have four reasons for this request: First, these people can sense how you are feeling about them. Second, they are probably more complex as human beings than that single opinion illustrates. Third, it is within the realm of possibility that you are misunderstanding them. Fourth, they might offer you information or a perspective that you are currently lacking.

You certainly don't have to agree with ideas or ideologies that don't appeal to you. But an emotionally intelligent way to manage these situations is to replace your leap to judgment with *curiosity*—a desire to find out why this person thinks the way he or she does. Judgment kills relationships; curiosity builds them.

Imagine, for example, that you've met someone who supports a political candidate you do not approve of. Instead of leaping to what might be a natural response—"That's crazy. You're wrong"—you might instead say, "I don't understand how you could think that your candidate is better than mine, and I want to. What is it about your candidate's policies, background, or agenda that impresses you? What do you think your candidate can do for the country that my candidate can't?"

In an interview with Henry about high-performing teams and leadership, former fighter pilot and two-time astronaut Sid Gutierrez eloquently expressed an idea that we endorse. Part of Henry's preparation for this interview was to ask his Facebook friends, "What would you ask an astronaut if you had the chance?" Sid agreed to answer some of those questions and asked, "Is the first question about aliens?" Henry said, "Yes it is!" They both smiled, and Henry asked, "While in space, have you ever seen anything that you could not explain?"

Sid leaned in and said, "No; but I think that most people in the world would fit into one of two primary categories on the subject of aliens. The first group claims to have had direct encounters with aliens through sightings, abductions, and so forth. The second group thinks that the first group is crazy or stupid. I'm in a third category, which I believe to be a minority: that there might be an entire world of knowledge that we don't have at this point in our understanding as a species. People may have witnessed or seen things that cannot be explained or categorized because they could fall under the category of a realm that we cannot and do not even begin to understand. In the end, I believe that there might be plenty I don't know. I try to remain open to that possibility when I meet people with different opinions from my own."

Sid reiterates our underlying point: people cannot be defined *exclusively* by one opinion. Therefore, we must remain open to other possibilities beyond our current level of understanding.

Imagine someone in a business setting offering a course of action that you don't like: "I think we should liquidate the parts division and focus instead on selling complete systems through dedicated retail stores." Rather than leaping to judgment of their proposal, you might ask a question such as, "I don't see how selling high-end systems in a down economy will help secure our future over the next few years. I am interested in hearing more about how you think it will."

Suppose that the other person is getting angry during this confrontation. What if you were to take a moment to contemplate how that person feels? Is he or she angry or feeling threatened? Do you know what it is like to feel that same way? Can you find compassion—and how do compassion and understanding feel on a physical level? Do you feel better already? Lighter? Breathing more easily? If so, then that is the energy you will project during this confrontation—which will make you much more likely to have a positive effect on the other person's emotional state as well. One of Henry's favorite proverbs is, "Hating someone is like swallowing poison and waiting for that other person to become sick."

Managing Your Emotions

The feelings you experience are preceded by physiological changes in your body. Afflictive emotions might make your chest and jaw tight, your breathing shallow, your hands clench into fists, and your shoulders tense. In other words, your body always gives you a heads up that you are about to realize a feeling. Becoming angry is your body giving you a sign that you are about to go primal. When you sense that this process is beginning, use the following techniques to help you stay intelligent.

Breathing

Deep, controlled breaths help restore blood flow and stop the production of the chemicals that cause you to react suddenly and with great force. Sometimes it is hard to take a deep breath when upset. In those moments, try breathing *out*. Do it now.

Breathe all the air out through your mouth, and you will notice that you cannot help but take a deep breath in.

Of course, breathing out through your mouth may work well while sitting alone and reading this book. It may not work quite as well when sitting at a meeting or a dinner table surrounded by other people who are looking at you. So try an alternative for those situations. Slowly push the air out of your lungs through your nose. Again, you will notice that you can't help but breathe in afterwards. Really, try it now. We promise you will have more oxygen available to you after you breathe out.

Questioning

When you ask your brain a question—any question—it forces blood back into the neocortex where intelligent thought occurs. Your body stops producing the "bad" chemicals and restores your ability to think and act more rationally. So ask yourself a question when you are triggered—and start simple: *What did I eat for breakfast yesterday? What is the last good movie I saw? What time did I wake up yesterday?*

Although any question will produce the desired result of a calmer emotional state and more rational thinking, you can ask more sophisticated questions appropriate to the situation at hand as you progress in this practice. *What can I say to make this other person feel safe right now? What am I really trying to accomplish in this situation? What can I say or do to build this relationship?*

Palms Up

You may notice that when you are triggered, you put your palms down or cross your arms. Uncross your arms and focus on keeping your palms in an open and up position, even if you are on the phone.

Time-Out

Sometimes all the techniques and leadership approaches in the world aren't going to help because you're simply too stressed. In these moments, we suggest that you politely exit the situation. Admit your own feelings to yourself and, without blaming the other party, remove yourself until you can find balance. You might explain, "I know I'm not capable of discussing this rationally right now, and I request that we revisit it tomorrow."

•••

Managing your emotions in the moment is not always easy. It requires practicing these techniques when you're *not* in such moments so that they are readily available to you when you are. Anger will probably require the most practice. Also bear in mind that you leave yourself open to being hijacked if you are someone who cannot handle negative emotion. That is, it's easier for others to put you in a negative mood—and at a disadvantage. Certain people are good at spotting your triggers and can use them against you if you are not able to leverage your negative emotion.

Plan for the times that you expect to be irritated, and rehearse the responses we have suggested. Remember that your body will give you a heads up. If you are aware of what is happening in your body, you can interrupt the cycle, stay at the stage in which you are simply irritated, and not let the emotion get out of hand.

When you are in control, you are able to observe and appropriately control your own behavior, either allowing the anger to build or dampening your response. Psychologist Maureen Gaffney explains this as the difference between saying "I am angry" and saying "I have the experience of being angry" or, more simply put, "I am feeling angry." In this way, you are asserting that your emotion is not the whole of you.[3]

Leveraging Anger

Anger is a potentially toxic emotion. The techniques we described will help you get in control of it and remain intelligent. However, the point is not to calm down but to hold on to the high-energy state that you are in, recognize that it can be useful, and direct it toward something productive. Redirect your anger into constructive activity. When you are in control, you are able to respond appropriately.

One example of doing this involves an employee who was putting her job in jeopardy. She was consistently late for meetings and dismissive of the subject matter during the meetings because, as she explained, "I don't give a damn about this topic. It doesn't affect me and I'm already overworked, so why should I take my time to go into this meeting full of people I'm not connected to and deal with their crap?"

This employee's supervisor saw that she was missing the connections between her work and others'—specifically, that they shared some financial incentives. The supervisor also wanted to repair the very low level of trust on the team, which required the employee's presence.

The supervisor was coached to leverage his justifiable anger about the employee's behavior and attitude. He told her, "I am very frustrated and angry that I am going to have to fire you in thirty days if your behavior does not change. Picture us sitting down in this room in thirty days, both really upset and frustrated that we failed because you have not been willing to show up to these meetings on time." Ultimately, the employee did not improve her attitude or behavior and was released by the company. She felt that she had been treated fairly, for the most part, and the supervisor gained a lot of credibility with the rest of the team for resolving what was perceived to have been an "old problem."

A second example of using anger productively involves the CFO of a financial institution who first had to stop *suppressing* his anger. One of his employees had a child sick with leukemia; she sometimes didn't come to work and often left early. When she was there, she didn't do a whole lot of work, and the rest of the team was running around her and beginning to miss their targets. They could not afford to carry a passenger, but they were all trying to do just that.

When the CFO thought about the problem, he allowed himself to feel only compassionate toward the woman; he had never allowed himself to be angry. As we worked with him, he began to let this happen. He never expressed his anger to her, but did allow it to rise without feeling guilty about it. Then he started to see the reality of the situation: that she was incapable of ever coming back to work and that his team couldn't continue to work the way they were. He had to have an honest conversation with her about her role on the team.

Acknowledging his anger allowed him to reach beyond his compassion, stop seeing himself as a bad guy, and offer her a different role in the organization. It turned out that she did not *want* a full-time, all-day, five- or six-days-a-week job. She was actually happy and relieved that somebody had the guts to treat her as a grown-up and not tiptoe around the issue of her child's illness, and preferred to work part-time so that she could care for her child.

When the CFO kept his anger buried and allowed himself to feel only compassion, he saw only one set of solutions. When he *did* get angry, he saw a different set of solutions. And once he gained control of his anger, he still had the ideas that came to him in his angry state. The anger-induced ideas weren't necessarily better, but using both compassion and anger gave him more options.

Although it is important to be able to use the energy your anger produces, many leadership moments show up as opportunities to **challenge others** to make a choice about what *they* are going to do in a heightened state of negative emotion. You do need to be able to be angry yourself so that you are comfortable with that emotion. This way, you do not freak out, shrink, or run away when other people are angry in your presence. You can help them redirect it when you have developed some skill at recognizing and dealing with your own emotions by practicing the techniques described earlier in this chapter. If you have done that, you will immediately recognize the opportunity to lead when you see anger in people around you—and you can become a catalyst for positive action.

Supermarket Sensitivity

Leadership moments often show up when you are working in a group—and you can take those opportunities whether you are the formal leader or simply a member. To do so, it helps to understand how various emotions influence groups as they work on specific tasks.

David Caruso, a leading researcher in emotional intelligence, has developed a useful way of looking at people's various emotions in a group setting, and how they can use them for the tasks that groups perform (see Figure 1.2).

Sometimes you want people angry in order to drive the best business result. You may also wish to catalyze a spectrum of emotions, focusing on certain ones during particular stages of a process or project. For example, imagine that you're facilitating a decision-making meeting. Ideally, everyone will be in the top right-hand quadrant (Figure 1.2) at the start, feeling high-energy and positive. In this mood, people are open to possibilities, and they readily see opportunities and generate lots of ideas. Once they've voiced these ideas, they will then need to organize them and agree on priorities. The bottom right-hand

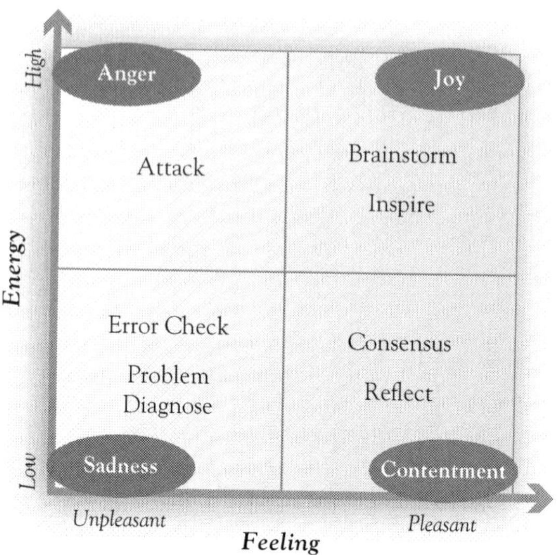

Figure 1.2 Mood and Cognition Model
Copyright © Dynamic Results, LLC; adapted from the work of David Caruso

quadrant is the most appropriate mood for this phase. People remain positive, but the energy level drops as they reflect on their work and move toward a consensus.

Next they need to assess the risks involved in their decisions, asking such questions as, "Have we picked our best ideas?" "What might go wrong?" and "What contingencies do we need to plan for?" The bottom left-hand quadrant of the Mood and Cognition model is now the optimal mood, as this is where the emotional brain is warning of danger out there—and telling you to tread carefully and wisely.

Finally, it comes time to stop the analysis phase of the decision-making process and generate the energy and confidence to move to action. This is a leadership moment in which someone might step up and say something like, "Everyone knows we are at very high risk if we don't make the right choice here, so let's focus."

Perhaps more than any other emotion, anger creates an urge to move and will propel the group to take action.[4] It also narrows the group's focus and increases its confidence. When the group is ready to execute its plan, anger will help to end any further search for solutions and prevent paralysis by analysis.

Remember: anger isn't necessarily a useful emotion in which to *develop* plans. But once you have a plan, you can use anger in an emotionally intelligent way to implement it.

There is an **optimal mood for every task** that a group might undertake. Knowing this provides you with leadership opportunities, in that you can help *create the mood.* Doing so requires that you become sensitive to the moods of those around you and develop your own repertoire of things that you might do or say to affect those moods.

It can be a challenge to perceive others' moods; however, it's usually easier than we think. Imagine that you're in line at a supermarket behind just one or two people. You are close enough to see the conveyer and other people's groceries, but you haven't been able to put your own purchases down yet. Can you tell what mood the cashier is in, even though he or she is not speaking to you yet? Are you able to determine what kind of day that cashier is having? Can you tell by the shape of the cashier's mouth, the look in the eyes, the posture, and the tone of voice? People around you are giving you the gift of clues to how they are feeling in the moment. You just need to be tuned in to them. In fact, dogs are excellent at reading human facial expressions, and some research indicates that when you are reprimanding a dog, it is not your voice but your facial expression that it is primarily responding to. (You probably know someone who is not as evolved as a dog, but that is a subject for an entirely different book.)

Almost everyone says yes to our questions about the supermarket checker; almost everyone is able to sense others' moods. So why are they so apt to miss the moods of people they work with every day when they are with them in a meeting? Is it because they are a little more relaxed in a supermarket checkout line where there is not much at stake? Or is it simply that they are blind to the importance and role of others' emotions in a professional setting? You must also be aware that *you yourself* are the cashier; others can see how you are really feeling when you are interacting with them, so you might as well leverage those feelings. If you can enter a meeting in a more relaxed state, you can then gauge how other people are feeling. Being sensitive to others' moods is simply a matter of being relaxed—that is, less self-conscious—and deciding to pay attention to them.

In Position to Lead

Armed with awareness of a group's mood and tasks, you are in position to lead in one of two ways. First, you can **leverage the existing mood** by introducing a task that meets that type of mood. Imagine that you are with a group that has recently experienced a failure, just like the client we discussed at the beginning of the chapter. Your group has worked for some months to retain a reluctant client who eventually left. Now another opportunity is on the horizon, but everyone is still suffering emotionally from the loss. This is a great time to diagnose why you lost the client. You can make optimum use of the unpleasant mood and low energy by saying something to the group like, "Hey guys—this really sucks, and I'm as upset about it as you are. But *how* did we lose this client? What exactly did we do—or fail to do?" We all know that Albert Einstein defined insanity as doing the same thing over and over and expecting a different result. By asking questions like these, you challenge the group to acknowledge behaviors or business practices that create self-inflicted pain, and, well, knowledge is power. Now you have something to work on.

Another one of our clients provided a second example of introducing a task to leverage a mood. On Friday afternoons, after about 3:00 P.M., this company allows its employees to open beer and wine in the office and just hang out. Nobody gets loaded, but they relax, wind down, and talk with one another. They enter into that relaxed, low-energy mood in the lower right-hand quadrant of Caruso's model.

Your organization may not "bust out the booze" on Fridays and may even have a formal policy against doing so. With or without booze, though, the end of the workweek is a great time to ask such questions as, "What do you think we did best in the past week?" "What process improvement could we make so that our wins would be easier to accomplish?" or "What did we learn this week [about the client, ourselves, and so on]?" You might get fifty ideas in that moment, because people are so open and relaxed. To set the mood, and in lieu of liberating people's creativity with drink, you might say something like, "It's been a long week and we've accomplished a lot as a team, [insert your reflective question here]."

Another approach is to **change the mood** so that it is appropriate to a required task. Let's continue with the example of the group that's in a down mood because of having lost a client. Rather than leveraging that mood, you can use your own energy, enthusiasm, and words to move the group into a high-energy and pleasant state. You could say something such as, "We are all feeling bad about our loss, but our lives are not over. We have a potential client giving us a chance to earn all of their business. Can we come up with one breakthrough idea to capture this opportunity? The people in this room are smart enough and creative enough to do that."

Keep in mind that using this model does not mean asking, "Which one of these four moods do I want people in on a Monday morning?" This is a futile approach; you need to know the *context*. What is the group trying to accomplish? What does the next challenge look like?

If you can neither leverage the existing mood nor change it, simply acknowledge that this is not a leadership moment for you. It happens. Don't worry about it; just look for the next opportunity.

Questions, Questions, Questions

We will close this chapter with seven questions. You should ask yourself the first three before an interaction that you suspect might raise negative emotions.

- How am I feeling right now?
- Why I am feeling this way?
- What emotions am I primed to experience because of my background mood?

Get really good at asking these questions. Do not let yourself off the hook with superficial answers like, "I just do."

The next two questions will help you manage your emotions during the moment in which they occur.

- Are my emotions intensifying?
- Am I choosing to *allow* my emotions to heighten, or are *they* now in charge?

Be mindful of what is going on inside you in these moments. Practice this skill frequently so that you can stay engaged in the conversation while also monitoring your emotional reaction in real time.

The final questions will help you redirect the emotion toward a positive end.

- What would be a good use of the energy I am feeling right now?
- What could my next step be?

For instance, you might be able to use the energy to tackle a piece of work you have been putting off. If you have been delaying a difficult conversation, use the energy to dial the number; your anger will naturally dissipate once you are dialing. If you are sad, proofread an important document; check the calculations in a key financial analysis. If you are happy, take out twenty Post-it notes and write down the first twenty ideas that come to mind.

•••

A lot of human behavior results from the way we are wired. Our behavioral patterns have formed strong neural pathways in our brains. However, the good news is that our brains *are* changeable.[5] With effort and the right techniques, we can form new pathways and patterns and alter our automatic responses. Practice the techniques we have presented in this chapter, and you can create new ways of thinking, even when you are angry, and you will produce better outcomes for you and others.

Summary of Key Learnings in Chapter One

- You can leverage your negative emotions to produce positive outcomes.
- The key to developing your ability to remain intelligent, even as your blood begins to boil, is to recognize that you're not

necessarily angry or not angry, but that there are many levels of anger.

- If you can remain aware of what is happening in your body, you'll stay at the stage in which you are simply irritated and not let the emotion get out of hand, until you develop the skill of handling more intense emotions.
- Stepping up in those moments in which other people are angry requires both the ability to make productive use of your own negative emotions and the skill to help others do the same.
- Knowing that there is an optimal mood for every task that a group might undertake provides you with leadership opportunities. You can step up to help create the mood.

Your Next Steps to Step Up and Use Anger Intelligently

- The first step to leveraging your anger is to identify your "triggers"—those people and circumstances that you've discovered are likely to anger you. Create a plan for the next time that you expect to be irritated, and rehearse a thoughtful response in lieu of a reaction.
- Identify the next key team meeting you are going to have. Determine what type of work the team will be engaged in and plan to create an appropriate mood (positive mood for creative tasks, negative mood for tasks that involve a search for potential error—for example, risk mitigation planning). Think through your personal repertoire of options for generating different moods in the group. Remember, moods are contagious—so getting in that mood yourself is the first step.
- Identify a recent setback that the team has faced. Challenge yourself as to whether you are using the resulting anger as fuel to drive the team forward. Plan to remind the team of how it felt to suffer a setback (without dwelling on it) and

focus them on what you all are going to do so that such a setback never happens again.

- When examining a setback or failed outcome, go outside first: "What external forces and entities contributed to our loss?" After you've completed that, go inside: "How did we help create our own monster? What could we have done differently or better? What will we do differently next time?"

Step Up Link

Mood and Cognition Model

CHAPTER TWO

Avoid Terminal Politeness

Until we have real conflict, we don't fully understand the problem.
—*Alfred Sloan*

Our Promise

In many organizations, authentic, robust debate and challenge have been replaced by what we call *terminal politeness*. In this chapter, we will show you how to recognize leadership opportunities when people are being so polite that serious issues never come to the surface. We will show you what is going on during those moments and how to deal productively with conflicts that arise when you embrace constructive conflict.

Recognize the Moment

The CEO of the subsidiary of a major retail bank had been parachuted to his position by the head office when the previous—and much loved—CEO retired. Although the old CEO had been a charismatic business builder, he was a classic conflict avoider. The question of his succession had never been openly discussed with his key lieutenants, at least two of whom presumed that they were the CEO-in-waiting. Avoiding open discussion with his team protected the old CEO from the conflict that he knew the conversation would cause. He also developed and supported a culture of conflict avoidance in the organization, which made the situation difficult for his successor—who was not particularly comfortable with conflict either.

It seemed as though members of the top team were waiting for the new CEO to fail so that they could have a second run at getting the position. Performance began to suffer, and when the main bank itself ran into difficulties, the subsidiary was sold to a competitor. Although the subsidiary's loan book was relatively attractive to the acquiring company, not all of the employees were. Half of the staff and all of the executives were let go, including the CEO.

By avoiding challenging conversations, the retired CEO set the new CEO up for failure; and by failing to tackle the unresolved resentment, the new CEO allowed the top team to disintegrate, taking the subsidiary down with it.

People often avoid having the most important conversations, even when such avoidance can damage their organization or their careers. They usually do so for at least four possible reasons:

- They don't feel emotionally safe having such conversations, because "messengers get shot."
- The organizational culture encourages people to be too nice.
- They aren't honest with themselves. They tell themselves things like, "I've been too busy to address the issue," instead of admitting, "I'm afraid to have that conversation."
- They think they're being considerate of someone else and "never find the right time" to have the discussion because

the other person is "too busy" or "having a hard time right now."

As consultants, we perform assessments, create development plans, and do development work with intact work teams. We often find that some of these teams avoid having robust, healthy debate and, when needed, healthy conflict. As we noted earlier, we refer to this avoidance as *terminal politeness*, meaning that people will tactfully dodge having the conversation they *should be having*. It is the same kind of behavior that we see when someone has a drinking or obesity problem. The people who care about the person are worried, but they don't want to hurt his feelings, so they "politely" enable his habits.

When people avoid these tough conversations, they spend most of their time and energy focused on what other people are doing wrong—yet are unwilling to comment on it. And though that's where the problem begins, it is not at all where the problem ends. In Henry's previous book, *Winning with Accountability*, he wrote about "passive endorsement" as a form of destructive behavior. This occurs when someone is aware of something bad happening; she may even comment on it to people who cannot effect change. But because she is not speaking directly to the people who can do something about the problem, she makes it worse—and her passive behavior invites it to continue. We often tell people in our workshops that failing to address a problem is almost the same as writing about the problematic behavior on a card, sticking the card in an envelope, sealing the envelope, applying postage, and mailing it to people as a way of inviting them to continue.

We would like you to take a moment right now and consider what is happening in your own organization. What are some conversations that you or others should be having but that you are avoiding for the sake of harmony? Which debates should you be having that you or others have decided are just not worth it, figuring that it is best just to keep the peace? If there are such conversations or debates, you may have a terminal politeness problem.

While we were writing this book, a South Korean airliner, Asiana Flight 214, crashed at the San Francisco International Airport. In many cultures, including the Korean culture, it is considered impolite to correct or offer constructive criticism to one's superior—a cultural norm that may very well have played a role in this scenario. There was ample evidence and plenty of data letting the flight team know that they were on a bad approach to the runway; but for some reason, no one warned the pilot. As a result, 3 people died, and 181 were injured.

People who regularly engage in terminal politeness tend to have good intentions. However, the result of their tact is a failure to openly hold important debates. They may allude to these matters around the watercooler or leave them to fester until they reach a crisis point and become personal and nasty. Needing to deal with a high-stakes, high-risk disagreement is a classic example of a potential leadership moment that, when not seized, often turns destructive.

Optimizing Conflict

Avoiding conflict also takes a toll on innovation. Consider the following three questions:

- Is your organization under increasing pressure to *do more with less?*
- Do you wish that your organization or team were better at coming up with *innovative or novel ways* to solve the most difficult problems that you face?
- Consider the top two or three things that your *organization could improve*. Is innovation on that list?

If you answered yes to any of these questions, then you may have an innovation deficit in your organization. Many leaders struggle with this issue because they don't quite understand the nature of negative emotion, conflict, and tension. We have all seen images of creative work spaces, with staffers in shorts and sneakers lounging around on beanbags, and have thought, "If only my environment were that fun and playful. We would be much more innovative."

It is absolutely true that positive emotions are conducive to generating novel ideas, but that is not the whole story. Your organization may lack innovation not because your environment is not fun enough but because you're not generating the right type of conflict. Our clients often talk about igniting the "spark of innovation." But you need friction to ignite sparks. Without healthy and productive conflict, you can't generate friction. Simply put,

no conflict = no friction = no sparks

The challenge then is to ignite enough of the **right type of conflict** to bring the best out of people. In his best-selling book *Death by Meeting,* Patrick Lencioni maintains that meetings should be like movies; that is, they should have drama. We embrace Lencioni's thinking and expand this concept to all relationships and to some of our interactions.

Many of today's organizational leaders avoid conflict because they've been trained to build *cohesion* in teams. They have attended the Outward Bound type of team-building exercises, done the "trust falls," and have come away from it all with the misguided impression that their job is to ensure that the team "gets along"—and that the more cohesive and connected the team, the better the result. As participants and also as outside observers, we have witnessed the type of team-building activities that we like to refer to as "edutainment." All the participants have a fantastic time—but they don't create any kind of operating agreements that would lead to sustainable and positive behavioral change for the organization. You do not optimize team performance by limiting conflict. In fact, the relationship between conflict and team performance is curvilinear.[1] Figure 2.1 illustrates this "conflict parabola."

Note that performance rises as conflict rises—*up to a point*. Then it drops as conflict becomes dysfunctional. Yes, it is important to be wary of conflict; misused, it can be a destructive force. However, too little conflict and too much conflict *both* obstruct performance. We've found that most organizations stay too far to the left on the curve—remaining in the terminal politeness zone, limiting conflict and thus performance. They're generally afraid of what might happen if conflict were to get out of hand. And even though they're right to be cautious, most of the organizations we've worked with could stand to ramp up

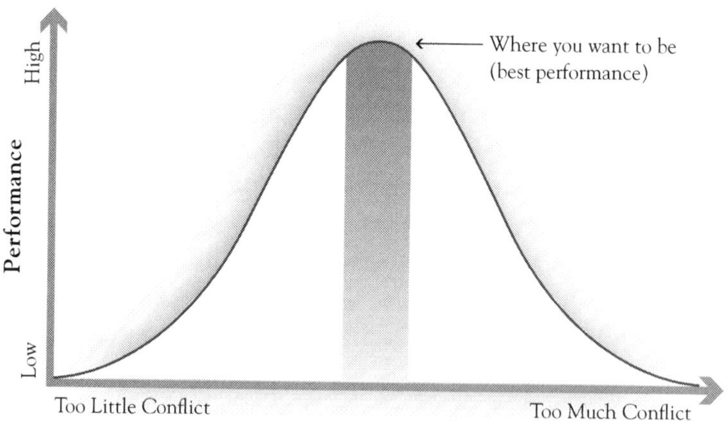

Figure 2.1 The Conflict Parabola
Copyright © Dynamic Results, LLC

the level of constructive conflict quite a bit before they got to the point where it would become destructive.

We worked with a senior leadership team of a creative agency that was having real problems. The executives had tried team building and personality profiling for the team, but the relationships on the team still seemed to be in terminal decline. The CEO of the agency came to us and asked us to help. When we attended a team meeting, we noticed that they were very polite, but that there was an unmistakable undercurrent of tension, which was strangely unspoken. When we coached team members one-on-one, we noted that there were a number of unresolved issues between team members and between the members and the CEO. These issues were not being addressed for fear of the conflict that might result.

One of the killers of high-performance teamwork is "unfinished business." We helped the members recognize and deal with their conflicts, and, once they started to be real with each other, the tensions began to subside and the performance of the team improved.

One instance in particular was very powerful. Jean-François was the leader of the digital media team, and he reported to the CEO. One of Jean-François's staff had to be fired due to malfeasance, and Jean-François raised the issue with the CEO, who curtly told him to handle it himself. Jean-François felt that the CEO had failed to support him on this sensitive personnel matter. He told us, "I have lost respect for that guy, but there is no way I am raising the issue so that he can speak to me like that again."

Jean-François and the CEO's interactions became excessively polite and "professional" in order to avoid any genuine contact that might lead to interpersonal conflict. After some coaching with both Jean-François and the CEO, they had a meeting in which they discussed their feelings about "the incident." Jean-François honestly explained how let down he had felt, and the CEO openly accepted that he had not been as supportive as Jean-François would have liked. He offered a genuine apology. Jean-François now says that the relationship is much stronger than it would have been even if the CEO had responded perfectly in the first place.

We have certainly worked with teams that are on the opposite end of the parabola. Those teams have members who seem to feel that causing disruption and conflict is the best way for them to contribute value to the team and to the organization as a whole. They wind up inciting conflict for the sake of conflict and, in doing so, create an environment in which other people feel emotionally unsafe, causing them to shut down and to stop contributing.

So what's your job? To see your team achieve greatness, you will need to consistently strike the balance point where you and your team enjoy an optimal level of conflict. You probably have strong relationships in your life that are even stronger as a result of having navigated some adversity. The two of us experienced some adversity while writing this book and gained a much deeper understanding of each other as a result. Colm would have his portion of the writing done very early in the production process. Henry felt pressured by Colm's always being out in front, and, as a result, he felt as though he was being rushed. Colm felt a bit of resentment and nervousness around Henry's apparent need to "wait until the last minute." After discussing the situation, we realized that Colm does his best thinking far in advance of a deadline, and Henry does his best thinking when coming up against that same deadline. Once we reached that mutual understanding, we could appreciate the other person's style instead of resenting it.

If you fail to understand the value of conflict and consistently slip into terminal politeness, your organization can't reap the benefits of a diverse workforce. Many organizations have embraced diversity on a superficial level and now have more diversity in their ranks in terms of gender, age, race, nationality, and so forth. However, some of those organizations then "manage the diversity out of people" by using standard practices, procedures, and protocols to the point where everyone ends up looking at opportunities and challenges in a standard "company way." We know of one organization that looks like the United Nations from the outside. However, if you talk to the individual staffers for more than five minutes, you realize that on the inside, they are all the same person—which completely misses the point of having a diverse workforce.

The best organizations aren't filled with drones. They are filled with a diverse group of people who leverage their diversity in a collaborative way. Pixar has produced some of the top-grossing films of all time. Part of their secret sauce is staffing their functional teams with a mix of older, very experienced people and younger, far less experienced people. They have found that the balance of mature wisdom with less mature and unbridled enthusiasm leads to the best forms of innovation.

Diversity is supposed to incite friction and conflict. Not simply tolerating but rather embracing that conflict is the source of any diversity dividend there is to be had in organizations. If your diverse workforce is not causing you headaches in terms of managing the differing opinions and values that the various individuals hold, you may be suppressing some conflict and losing the potential innovation benefit that comes with dealing with that conflict in a constructive way.

Building a shared identity and strong culture is hugely important. However, you can't let that restrict the flow of diverse and conflicting opinions. Truly innovative teams amplify differences in perspectives, expertise, and intentions, and use them as resources.[2] Innovation guru Peter Senge has challenged the consensus culture in organizations by saying, "We think agreement is so important. Who cares? You have to bring paradoxes, conflicts, and dilemmas out in the open, so collectively we can be more intelligent than we can be individually."[3]

The Need to Be Liked

People avoid conflict due to two fundamental needs: the need to be liked and the need to be right. Human beings are social animals; we're designed to be with other people and to operate in groups, communities, and societies. Our emotional brain is an *open loop system*, one designed to both transmit and receive emotional signals from the people around us.[4] We are therefore hardwired to make connections and to form an impression of what other people are thinking, especially about us.[5] In order for us to feel connected to other people, it is important for us to feel some degree of *resonance* with them—that is, that we like them and feel liked by them to some extent.

This idea of resonance is so fundamental that it even operates at the physical level. If you adopt the same poses and use the same gestures as another person, she will more readily agree with what you are saying because you are giving her physical cues.[6]

The next time you are in a busy restaurant, look at the body language of the couples around you. Try to spot the ones who are resonant and those who are not. Do their body positions mirror each other? Are they speaking with similar levels of animation? Do they maintain eye contact? Try not to focus excessively on specific details, but simply allow yourself to notice their energy. Does it feel warm or cold to you? You could also do this at your next team meeting. Try to spot the subgroups that are in alignment by noticing how they interact with and greet each other as they join the meeting.

Have you ever walked into a room just after two people have been fighting? That feeling in the air or the shiver down your spine is the way that you *physically* pick up on a lack of resonance between the two people. Your cognitive system then tries to make sense of the feeling by spotting the clues that something odd has just happened between them.

Another way to feel resonance—or the absence of resonance—is to conduct the following thought experiment. Let's take our two people who were fighting in the room. Let's presume that they had not been fighting, but instead had been talking about *you* in a not very flattering way. Now imagine that you walk into the room. How long do you think it would take you to realize that you were the subject of the interrupted conversation? What would that feel like? If this has ever actually happened to you, you may even *now* be feeling some residual anger, embarrassment, or shame. Even if it has never happened to you, you can probably experience viscerally what that must be like. The need to be liked, to be included and accepted, is indeed one of our most powerful needs.

There is considerable evidence that we like others better—that is, resonate with them more easily—the closer they resemble us on important qualities.[7] Research into how highly we rate others' capabilities and even the type of people we recruit into our organizations points to the fact that we regard people more highly when they are similar to us in some important way.[8] Researchers have even found that venture capitalists are more likely to invest in the projects of people with backgrounds similar to theirs, regardless of the objective financial merit of the business case presented to them. The similarity might be a matter of simple demographics, such as age, gender, or race, but also operates at the level of attitudes, beliefs, and personality.[9] When people hold opinions similar to ours, we presume that they hold similar attitudes, beliefs, and values, and we like them better for it; we resonate with them. We tend to think that people who think like we do are smart people.

So, does it matter that you like some people in your organization better than others? Get out a piece of paper and do the following exercise:

1. Write down a list of the ten people with whom you interact most at work.
2. Now rank-order the list from one to ten, from whom you like best to whom you like least.
3. Take a good look at how you treat the people at the top versus the people at the bottom.

How much of your time do they get? Where do their projects feature on your agenda? Who is more likely to get the juicy assignment? Whom do you confide in about sensitive information? Who gets the best resources for their projects? Can you honestly say that your review of the budgets of the people at the bottom of that list is the same as for the people at the top? Most of us like to think that we treat everyone fairly and equitably, but you may get a surprise if you have compiled your list honestly.

Simply put, it is easier for us to figure out someone who appears to be like us. In doing so, we use the part of our brain that is associated with self-reflection. But when we try to figure out someone who is not like us, we have to engage in some higher-level processing. Because we tend to do what's easier, we're apt to surround ourselves with people who resemble us.

There is also the following sobering thought: we tend to react most strongly to others' characteristics that remind us of what we *don't like about ourselves*. Try to maintain a high level of curiosity when examining this issue; the phenomenon can present itself in subtle ways. We worked with a VP of a financial services organization who had a very strong personality. She made a point of always challenging others' performance and had a reputation as a really tough taskmaster. She said that what she objected to most in others was the tendency to let mediocre performance slide. However, she couldn't see how this was something about herself that she also judged.

She told us, "It really bugs me when the chairman doesn't hold the other VPs to account. I never ever do that, so it can't be something about me that I am reacting to in him." However, she realized after doing some development work that she did indeed have an inclination to be soft on performance—something she feared others would view as a feminine weakness in a masculine world. She had spent so long being tougher than her male colleagues that she had buried her natural tendency to be compassionate and nurturing deep inside her. As a result, she was overcompensating with a harsh approach to others' mistakes. We have consistently found that where a client has a strong objection to someone's behavior, there is a good chance that the other person reflects an aspect of the client's own character, however deeply buried that aspect is.

Take a moment and write down a metaphor for each member of your team at work (the shark, the owl, the lone wolf, the volcano, the monster, the rainbow child . . .). Now stand back and look at the metaphors you have used, ignoring the people you were describing. Is there a common theme? Have you used similar types of images? If you look very closely at the images you chose, you may find a thread that leads back to you. It will not be obvious. Remember, you are trying to hide this feedback from yourself, but if you deeply reflect, especially with the help of a good coach, you will discover a kernel of truth about yourself.

However, the real concern from an organizational perspective is not that we like people better when they are similar to us. Rather, it's that this tendency leads us to rate them more highly. You may think that this is just a feature of first impressions and that once you get to know the person, you base your evaluation of him on his objective performance. Unfortunately, this isn't often the case. We are all subject to something called the *Pygmalion effect*: the greater the expectation we have of people, the better we rate their performance. We are subject also to its opposite, the *Golem effect*; that is, our low expectations lead us to be skeptical of others' performance. (We are more likely to attribute it to luck, external circumstances, and so on.)[10] So the first impressions we form about others, based on liking or not liking them, influence not just how we view evidence about their performance. They also determine **what evidence we choose to focus on**—which in turn affects their performance.

So: we all like and tend to surround ourselves with people who are like us on important attributes—usually values, attitudes, and beliefs. We also tend to come up with explanations for the behaviors of people not like us that prevent us from feeling as though *we* need to change. For example, the tendency to say something like, "Well, all accountants are just bean counters, so of course I'm having a difficulty with the head of finance."

Just because lots of your friends agree with you doesn't make your position right. And the fact that you don't particularly like the people who disagree with you doesn't make it OK to dismiss their feedback.

The Need to Be Right

We also avoid conflict and withdraw into terminal politeness because we frequently *need to be right*.

When people agree with us, they are confirming that our opinions or decisions are accurate—and we all like being right. There is too much information available to us every minute of every day for us to take it all in. Therefore, we have become highly selective in what information we attend to and what we ignore. We are designed to seek out evidence that confirms our decisions and to ignore evidence that suggests we are wrong. We pay attention to some information, and our brains fill in the rest using our experience, memory, or expectation. The following famous experiment will help you see this in action. See if you can make sense of the following statement:

> I cdnuolt blveiee that I cluod aulaclty uesdnatnrd what I was rdanieg. The phaonmneal pweor of the human mind! Aoccdrnig to ____ at Cmabrigde Uinervtisy, it deosn't mttaer in waht oredr the ltteers in a wrod are; the only iprmoatnt tihng is that the fisrt and last ltteer be in the rghit pclae. The rset can be a taotl mses, and you can still raed it wouthit a porbelm. This is bcuseae the huamn mnid deos not raed ervey lteter by istlef, but the word as a wlohe. Amzanig, huh?

Get it? The paragraph is self-explanatory, but if it made no sense at all to you, have another look at it. Read it through fairly quickly. Your brain will focus on the shape of the word and maybe the first and last letter, and then work out the rest itself. The human mind seeks familiar patterns and, as the experiment shows, can create them even when there are big gaps in the data.

There's another factor that further complicates how our need to be right renders us terminally polite—something organizational psychologists call *self-serving bias*. This simply means that we explain our attitudes, behaviors, and decisions so as to make ourselves look and feel good, and we tend to diminish or explain away evidence that contradicts our beliefs.[11] Most people admit that it feels bad and embarrassing to be wrong. However, author Kathryn Schulz points out that people are in fact explaining what it feels like to *realize* that they are wrong. In fact, she says that the feeling of being wrong is exactly the same as the feeling of being right, up to the moment that you realize you are wrong.[12] Her counterintuitive insight is that the level of confidence or conviction you may feel is not a reliable gauge of the accuracy or veracity of your opinion. We base our decisions on our judgments and beliefs; and when they are flawed, they give us a false sense of confidence.

The more people disagree with us, the more we associate them with dissonance, the less we like them, and the lower we rate their capabilities. The heart of the problem lies in our failure to adequately distinguish between the person and the idea. Furthermore, as mentioned in the book *Sway: The Irresistible Pull of Irrational Behavior,* we sometimes have a "diagnosis bias"—in other words, the moment we label a person or situation, we put on blinders to all evidence that contradicts our diagnosis.[13]

Go back to the list of your ten colleagues that you made earlier in this chapter. Imagine that you have a new idea about a project at work. Who is more likely to agree with your idea, the person at the top or the person at the bottom? Now imagine a person whom you really don't like at all. What would her response to your idea be? As we noted earlier, it is a normal human tendency to like people who agree with us and to dislike people who disagree with us. "But the reason I like them is that they ***have*** good ideas." Most people respond that way. We offer you the suggestion that one of the reasons that you like their ideas is that they have ideas that are like yours. If you can step back from this exercise, you may notice the circular and self-referential logic that is at play here. We want you to catch yourself saying or thinking that and recognize that you are presenting the concept that you like the person as a subjective opinion, but you are presenting the concept that they produce good ideas as an objective fact. Please remember all the reasons we discussed so far in this chapter which suggest that your "facts" are not nearly as objective as you think.

We hold people personally responsible for their decisions and actions to a greater extent than we should by not adequately allowing for external factors.[14] When a person creates conflict, presents difficult challenges, or argues for contentious ideas, most people will hold them personally responsible for the resultant conflict and will like them less and rate them lower because of that. People in organizations figured this out a long time ago. This is the reason for the "go along to get along" attitude, where debate and challenge are suppressed and the needs to be liked and be right rule, resulting in a dangerous false harmony.

On our best day, we might begin to appreciate people who alert us to alternative points of view. When we keep an open mind, we can understand that they present us with learning opportunities that the people who always agree with us do not deliver.

Step Up

You may never get to the point where you enjoy having your ideas challenged. However, all of us can certainly become better at keeping conflict from becoming destructive by learning how to skillfully distinguish between conflict with a person and **conflict about his or her idea**. Once you do this, you can learn how to avoid terminal politeness and achieve the optimum conflict level that will bring about successful ideas and solutions.

You want to seize moments where you can step up and exercise leadership by helping both yourself and others avoid the trap of terminal politeness. At the same time, you can engage others in making productive use of conflict. Attacking ideas without attacking the people who have those ideas is an art. The following examples offer you some basic brushstrokes.

Be Curious

Think about the last time you met someone with a radically different political, religious, or social opinion from your own. Were you a little too quick to label this person as "stupid"? Most of us have made this mistake at some point. Someone else's opinion or, worse yet, our *interpretation* of his or her opinion, caused us to rush to a judgment.

Kathryn Schulz spent five years studying how adults experience and respond to being wrong. She asserts that when we meet people who don't think like we do, we automatically assume that they are ignorant. We believe that once we "enlighten" them with our "facts," they will see things our way. When that doesn't work, we begin to assess them more harshly and characterize them as "stupid." If they still persist in thinking differently even after we've made our third attempt to persuade them, we assume that they must be "evil"; now they have all the information they need in order to think like we do, yet they continue to believe in the "wrong" thing.[15]

Nowhere in this scenario do we consider the possibility that *we may be wrong.*

We suggest that you seek people who have radically different opinions from your own. Instead of trying to convince them to see things your way, make it your goal to *understand them*. Seek to **understand before being understood**.

Focus on Transforming Yourself

Psychologist Robert Kegan offers an alternative way of approaching a disagreement:[16]

- Consider that the conflict is a signal that you and your opponent have probably identified with opposite poles.
- Consider that what you believe to be true may not seem true to others.
- Value the relationship, miserable though it may feel, as an opportunity to live out your own multiplicity.
- Focus on ways to let the conflict transform the parties rather than on ways for the parties to resolve the conflict.

The goal is to discover how you might be contributing to problems before you begin to blame others. Sometimes the very act of blaming is a warning sign that you need to take an introspective and self-reflective moment to see what your own role in the problem is. For example, have you been giving passive endorsements? Have you allowed something to build up to the point that it has become a big issue for you now—one that may soon cause you to "explode"? The other party probably does not understand what a big deal this is or has become, because you've never told him. In a case like this, you might approach him with an apology for not having brought this up sooner, rather than with an accusation and an attack about what he has been doing wrong.

Kegan's point is very powerful: conflict can be destructive when the parties involved become "ego-identified" with their positions. This happens when you stop thinking about the idea as an idea you happen to hold and start investing some of your personal identity with it—and see it as YOUR IDEA. Then you view the loss of the idea or argument as a threat to you as an individual.

Attack the Idea and Not the Person

It often feels as though we would be better liked if we got along with everyone in every situation. But are the people you respect most in the world likeable in every moment and interaction? When your intentions are good and you are not launching personal attacks, you can be quite assertive in challenging or disagreeing with people and ultimately still be liked, even if people have to struggle with you in certain moments.

If we lived in a world where everyone held the same political and social beliefs that we do, the weather was always to our liking, we never got sick or experienced traffic or pollution, maintained all relationships in a highly functional state, and enjoyed our desired state of health, we would all be nice people. We'd be easy to get along with, we'd be unlikely to challenge one another in a constructive way, and, as a result, we would create a spirit of complacency. The problem with this picture is that the spirit of complacency creates what we call a "fur-lined mousetrap": you become stuck, but in a comfortable place. If your competitors are better at having challenging and potentially conflictual discussions than you are, they will have a competitive advantage over you.

We teach our clients to become better at challenging another person's idea by thinking about the situation in terms of three points drawn onto a balloon. One point is you, another is the other person, and the third is the "contentious" idea. What happens when you squeeze two of the points together? The third gets pushed away. If you let yourself become ego-identified with the idea, you push the other person away and create the potential for conflict. You also leave so little space between you and your idea that there's no room for the other person to challenge the idea without taking a swipe at you. However, if you close up the (psychic) distance between you and the other person—and put some distance between yourself and the idea—you create resonance and limit your ego-identification with the idea. Even simple things can make a difference—for example, sitting on the same side of the table while looking at a presentation together, and taking turns explaining the benefits of the other person's idea. Be very conscious of how you run large meetings. By having everyone sit around the conference table while one team member stands and presents her idea, you physically reinforce the ego-identification with the idea. You can cause people to aggressively defend their idea because the situation you have created makes them feel threatened. Although people should defend their work and their opinions, creating an environment in which they feel threatened will limit effective conflict.

If as part of an effort to resolve a disagreement between you and a colleague, the colleague were presenting an idea to you, you could say something like this: "You and I have faced challenges like this before, and we have found creative ways to resolve them. In fact, I remember when we had to . . ." (Here you would cite a problem you solved together; this creates that sense of resonance we talked about.) "Now let's look at your current proposal. I can see how it addresses the financial problem, and I realize that you've worked hard at that part. However, I am still struggling to understand the market opportunity. Let's toss that one around a bit to see what we can come up with." By addressing your colleague's perspective in this way, you're able to demonstrate your appreciation for the person and his effort, while still challenging his idea. This approach may help prevent people from "taking things personally."

Later in this book, we will do a deep dive into how to explore an idea that's very challenging to hear. For now, let's look at what it might sound like when you hear an idea that is not in alignment with your own. You might use any variation of these statements that highlight **curiosity** rather than judgment:

> "I like your way of thinking, and your ideas are usually very creative. But I am really struggling with your current suggestion. What am I missing here?"

"I love working with you, and I'm having difficulty understanding the value of the idea you just offered. Here are some considerations I feel we should make before running with your idea. Can we explore those together?"

"I want to like your idea, and right now I don't. Would you help me understand why it makes sense for us?"

By asking questions such as these, you allow the other person to feel as if you respect her and are debating her ideas rather than judging her as a person because of her idea.

Really Listen

We often observe terminal politeness in teams that superficially display "good team" behaviors. They may have had some team coaching and know to listen respectfully when their colleagues are speaking; they no longer interrupt or speak over each other. However, being quiet—or quietly rehearsing your bit while another person is speaking—is not the same as *listening*.

We spot this behavior by playing back the meeting in our heads and asking, If we had changed the order in which people spoke, would the meeting have been any different? If the answer is no, then we wonder if people are really listening to each other, as the last person's perspective did not seem to alter what the next person said. Person A—who is just waiting for person B to finish speaking—might say something like, "I appreciate your perspective, but let me tell you how this issue is affecting my team." Person A does not actually appreciate person B's perspective; he just knows that he is supposed to use those words. He is going to give his team's unique perspective anyway.

A good way to change this behavior is to insist that person A summarize the perspective of person B's team before presenting his own team's perspective. But here is the catch—he must perform this summarization to person B's satisfaction. Person A cannot simply erect a straw man by twisting what person B said to suit what he wants or needs to say for his own purposes. When you paraphrase and reflect back to people what you have heard them say, they have to place a stamp of approval on your reflection in order for it to be valid.

Summarizing the last person's perspective before presenting your own helps you develop your ability to genuinely empathize with him or her. As a result, your meetings move beyond being a procession of terminally polite (yet potentially ego-identified) presentations.

Summary of Key Learnings in Chapter Two

- People often avoid having the most important conversations, even if this avoidance is damaging and potentially deadly to their organization or their careers.
- People tend to avoid conflict because they're seeking to fulfill two fundamental human needs: to be liked and to be right.
- It's easier to understand people who are like us than people who are not like us, so we tend to surround ourselves with people who resemble us.
- We often fail to adequately distinguish between a person and his or her idea. We can improve at not letting conflict become destructive by learning how to skillfully distinguish between conflict with a person and conflict about his or her idea. (Attack the idea, not the person.)
- When we paraphrase and reflect back to others what we have heard them say, they have to place a stamp of approval on our reflection in order for it to be valid.

Your Next Steps to Step Up and Avoid Terminal Politeness

- You can assess your team and also conduct an honest assessment of whether your organization has a "conflict avoidance" culture: Do you excessively value politeness? Are people who create conflict coached about how to behave properly? Do people complain about each other in subgroups outside of meetings? Is underperformance a difficult topic to broach? If you answered yes to any of these questions, you need to start to create some healthy conflict in your teams.
- Thinking in terms of the conflict parabola (Figure 2.1), identify the "sweet spot" of ideal conflict for an upcoming issue. Ensure that you have a good devil's advocate to present challenges to the team's suggestions.
- If you are the team leader, at the next team meeting in which you have to decide on a strategic issue, hear from everybody else before you give your opinion to ensure that people are not simply agreeing with the boss.
- Make a conscious effort to get to know the people at the bottom of your "People I Work With" list so that you can better appreciate their perspective. Do one thing this week to make that happen.
- Create a team protocol around attacking the idea and not the person. In your next team meeting, ask everyone to summarize the previous person's point before she can make her own. After the meeting, take time to discuss this practice. Did it work for the team? Did it allow you to move the conversation to a conclusion? (Remember, it will feel slower until you get good at it.)
- Print an idea in big, bold, 72-point type on a single sheet of paper, or use a single PowerPoint slide to get the idea up on a wall. Have the idea's advocate sit down with everyone else to discuss the merits and liabilities of the idea. Get everyone to speak.

Step Up Link

Video of the authors speaking about attacking the idea and not the person

CHAPTER THREE

Decide Already

The coward dies a thousand deaths, the brave but one.
—Ernest Hemingway

Our Promise

This chapter will help you understand how some people struggle to be decisive in challenging situations. We will give you the practical advice and tools you need to be convincing and decisive, even when dealing with highly uncertain situations. We will show you how to bring a style of leadership, which we call *decision leadership*, to the table when your team needs it.

Although this chapter discusses both productive and unproductive behavior that we have observed among people in formal leadership roles, the principles and suggestions that follow apply everywhere; there are certain moments that require people at *all* organizational levels to make decisions.

Recognize the Moment

We don't expect our leaders to be right all the time, as the only way to be right all the time is to constantly operate inside your comfort zone. We *do* expect them to be decisive and to be able to bring people along with them once they have made the call.

Whether they are conducting a difficult performance appraisal or implementing a company-wide restructuring decision, leaders make and communicate hard choices every day. And although they may seem completely confident and convinced of their position, many leaders face the same self-doubt and anxiety as those who don't consider themselves leaders.

Leaders aren't able to predict the future with 100 percent accuracy. They do not have perfect information or the luxury of the time and resources it takes to generate even near-perfect information. What they do have is the ability to decide on a course of action, commit to it, and then communicate that decision confidently and convincingly. Leadership, like courage, is not the absence of fear or doubt, but the ability to commit to a course of action in the face of both fear and doubt. Great leaders communicate honestly and transparently and make it clear to their followers that "we're all in this together." They exercise decision leadership, which we consider to be the ability to balance intuition with data and the ability to proactively take intelligent risks. When others are "stuck" or "frozen" in a state of indecision, the person who steps up and declares a decision is the leader in that moment or interaction.

You may be thinking, "If they are anxious but acting confident—how can this be honest?" The key is that great leaders truly commit to the decision, even though they are a little anxious, and honestly display an *authentic commitment*. They do not allow themselves the Get Out of Jail Free card of "I had my doubts all along" if things don't pan out as they'd hoped.

Don't Wait for Perfection

We have developed and executed strategies for our own organizations, consulted to many organizations on their strategies, and lectured to MBA programs on strategy and strategy execution. Although every instance is unique, we have found one truism: an 80 percent completed strategy brilliantly executed beats a 100 percent finished strategy badly executed. That is, as General George S. Patton said, "A good plan violently executed now is better than a perfect plan executed next week."

We have worked with plenty of organizations who got stuck in analysis paralysis while trying to complete a project. For example, we take our strategic planning and implementation clients through the very hard work of identifying their values, purpose, and vision for the future, and the challenges that would get in the way, and then determine all the strategic initiatives required to achieve this vision. At this point, they often want to reassess and reevaluate those initiatives rather than begin implementing them. We call this the *postponed perfection syndrome*: when an organization refuses to move to implementation until they have what they believe to be the "perfect plan."

Some estimates state that companies implement *less than 10 percent* of the actions written into their corporate strategic plans. Although others put the number as high as 30 percent, this is still abysmal. Our clients have on average an 86 percent implementation rate for their strategic plans—something they achieve by following the very specific implementation plan outlined in our Accountability Method™, even when outcomes are uncertain. They achieve greatness because they are willing to take action during unstable times when their competitors would rather play it safe by talking instead of *doing*.

Award-winning design and innovation consultancy IDEO has developed an approach to decision making by implementing plans that they refer to as *rough*, *rapid*, and *right*. Their philosophy is based on getting some type of prototype into consumers' hands as soon as possible and changing it quickly in response to consumer feedback. They don't worry about planning every detail up front, but instead concentrate on prototyping and amending quickly—an approach that has kept them at the forefront of innovative design for many years.

Spend some time with your team looking at the feedback that you are getting from customers (internal or external). Are issues being identified that you could have designed into the existing process if you had known about them earlier? Are you now struggling to retrofit changes based on "new" requirements from customers? In our experience, most "new" requirements could have been identified early on, if only we had codesigned the product with the users or customers. Ask yourself now what the best way is to find out about these issues sooner so that you can "fail early, fail cheap," as HP says.

True leaders know that there is no such thing as the perfect plan, no way of avoiding the need to exercise judgment, no amount of research or pilot studies that will make the decision for them. A key test of leadership arises when you are faced with a 51 percent to 49 percent call—when there are many good options or no good options—and you have to make a critical decision that may affect your organization's future for a long time to come. We like to make a distinction with our clients: they're not seeking 100 percent agreement when they're making a controversial decision; they're seeking 100 percent *understanding* that this is how they are moving forward. And they're confirming 100 percent commitment from their people to bring their highest capability and attention to the task.

You might say, "I'm not 100 percent sure that my decision will prove to be the correct one a year from now. However, everyone needs to be 100 percent sure that this is the direction we're going, and bring total commitment to the course of action. If it turns out to be wrong, OK. If you have to blame someone at that time, blame me. But because we all agree that we must make a decision now, we should all be clear that *this* is what we're doing."

There is an example of fully committing to a risky decision in one of our favorite movies, *Gladiator*. In the opening scenes, just before a battle in which the cavalry is about to play a vital and dangerous part, the general—Russell Crowe as Maximus—addresses the troops by saying, "Three weeks from now I will be harvesting my crops . . . imagine where you will be . . . and it shall be so. Hold the line. Stay with me. If you find yourself alone, riding in green fields with the sun on your face, do not be troubled; for you are in Elysium, and you're already dead! Brothers—what we do in life . . . echoes in eternity."

Maximus is facing a massive battle—one that may decide the outcome of the war, and one in which he is outnumbered and outgunned. This is a great example of having no good options as a leader. Having made his decision on the battle plan, he is now communicating his commitment to and belief in the plan. This is not the time for his troops to question his decision, to ask for more reconnaissance intel, or to reopen the debate as to the best course of action. This is the time to focus on brilliant execution of the plan. Maximus doesn't deny the inevitable casualties and is likely anxious because he is facing the same risk as his warriors. Yet he has clearly and confidently committed himself to the battle plan because that is what his warriors need from him in that moment.

This is not just an issue for those in formal leadership positions. Whatever your job title, nothing will undermine your leadership credibility more than the inability to make and *stick to* a decision that affects others. You may not technically hold a "leadership role," but there will nevertheless be times when people rely on you to make decisions.

Colm worked in a professional services firm with a senior partner for whom nobody wanted to work. They nicknamed him "Wishy-Washy" because he was so poor at making decisions, and they would go out of their way to avoid being on his team. His instructions were always vague, and it was impossible to get a straight answer from him. Naturally enough, his jobs rarely went to plan or to budget. As a result, the better trainees found ways to avoid being on his jobs, and he was left with staff who either didn't care or were incapable of getting allocated to more prestigious work. Naturally, Wishy-Washy's reputation for indecisiveness created a self-fulfilling negative prophecy.

We will talk later about instances when it is appropriate to change your decision; however, you should try to stick to the decisions you have made. We sometimes say that people who do not stick to their decisions suffer from *cushion syndrome*; that is, they bear the impression of the last person who sat on them! These leaders completely change their minds based on the last piece of input received. Working with someone like this can be exasperating.

The Why of Indecisiveness

The fact that any person who wishes to lead needs to be decisive and consistent is not a revelation. But if it's so obvious, what stops people—no matter what title they have—from being decisive in leadership situations? A number of factors can undermine your ability to decide, communicate, and execute in uncertain environments. We will deal with three of them here.

The first is that you may not even realize how often you do fail to face problems. You might think of yourself as a good decision maker, while others experience you as Wishy-Washy. We human beings are notoriously inaccurate in our ability to self-assess.

For example, Jen was a young marketing executive at a high-tech company. She was a "people person" who took a participative approach to problem solving and thrived in the company's collaborative, highly matrixed structure. Jen was selected to head up the organization's joint venture in Hong Kong with a local software firm. We met her six months into her assignment. She was deeply frustrated and felt that she was failing for the first time in her career.

Jen did not fully understand that the organizational (and national) culture in which she was operating was very hierarchical and had what psychologists call *high power distance*. That is, her staff expected *her* to make the decisions and saw her attempts to include them as a sign of indecisiveness. She was not deliberately, or even consciously, avoiding making decisions; she simply thought it valuable to get others' input. But her staff's perception of her impeded her success.

Once she was able to make a realistic self-assessment and come to terms with her team's expectations, she began to interact in a more directive way. Her staff developed more respect for her, and their performance improved. Jen has since made real progress in engaging others in joint decision making—something she's now doing from a position of credibility and strength rather than perceived weakness.

The crucial point of Jen's story is that it is very hard for people to truly understand their reputation for decisiveness. We suggest that you may be overestimating your own level of decision leadership—that is, your ability to take and commit to important decisions in uncertain situations—and urge you to get honest feedback from a trusted colleague to help you calibrate your performance in this area. If you haven't already done so, we also suggest that you take the online Step Up leadership self-assessment that we included in the Introduction to this book and pay close attention if your decision leadership score is average or low.

Try an experiment. If you are reading this in a place where there are other people—a coffee shop or an airport lounge, for instance—have a look at the people around you. Would you say that your IQ is above or below average in this group of people?

Research shows that 70 to 80 percent of people will report that they are above average. But less than 50 percent can be above average, so a lot of us are flattering ourselves in our self-assessments. In the numerous research studies that ask people to self-assess their IQ and then actually test the IQ, the correlation found is roughly 15 percent. And you get a lot of opportunities to assess your IQ; every test score you received in school or college is a piece of feedback on this. People seem especially immune to feedback when it comes to assessing their intellect. This is compounded by the fact that few of us rarely, if ever, get quality feedback on our leadership behaviors—leaving us with even less of a shot at developing a truthful self-assessment.

A second factor that keeps people from facing problems is they want to both *be and be seen as* a nice person. This is a phenomenon we refer to as a nurturing or positive bias. People with this bias believe in putting a positive spin on things and sharing bad news delicately and sensitively. They themselves tend to respond poorly to assertive and decisive people and can project that perspective onto others.

This attitude can dominate the culture of the entire organization. A few years ago, we conducted a research project with a major client. This organization had been at the top of its industry for many years, but was now facing a number of serious issues—mainly driven by changes in the economy—threatening both its performance and reputation.

The organization was failing to respond quickly enough to changes in its external environment. We always felt bad discussing this with our client, because they were such a joy to work with—always pleasant and polite. It was clear that they worked hard at valuing and being kind to their people.

And then we realized that this was part of the problem.

Seeing how nice they were to us made us realize that they were probably being this nice to each other and suffering from the terminal politeness described in Chapter Two. The company had been successful for so long, enjoying a near monopoly position, that it had evolved into an almost paternalistic culture. People didn't face up to problems or confront mediocre or even poor performance. No one was making the hard decisions, and even when someone did, those decisions were not communicated clearly and directly.

Contrast the politically correct platitudes of many of today's organizations with the message of a real leader, Ernest Shackleton, as demonstrated by the wording of the advertisement for men to accompany him on his Antarctic exploration that he is reputed to have placed: "Men wanted for hazardous journey. Small wages. Bitter cold. Long months of complete darkness. Constant danger. Safe return doubtful. Honour and recognition in case of success."

We have all heard that honesty is the best policy, and it is easy to be honest when you have a positive message to deliver. However, you can often be tempted to sugarcoat or downplay difficult information. You probably feel anxiety about your ability to make the point or intervention, and you worry about how people will receive the message. It's not that you doubt your ability to communicate the unpleasant message; you're just not sure that you can handle the associated anxiety.

This brings us to the third reason people struggle with making decisions. Many people simply doubt their ability, which can keep them from exercising leadership. We have taught leadership courses in MBA programs in the United States, Europe, and Asia, and have led leadership modules in-company for our clients. No matter where we are, what industry we are working in, or what level the participants are in their organizations, only a tiny minority of participants unequivocally claim that they are good leaders.

Even the leaders we deem great have to deal with self-doubt and anxiety when faced with crucial decisions—yet they find a way to communicate confidence and inspire others. Several years ago, we conducted a leadership workshop for senior leaders in Ireland. We invited Ned Sullivan, one of Ireland's most prominent business leaders, to talk to the group. Someone asked if he ever had doubts or regrets about the business decisions he had made in his career. Ned replied, "You have to learn to live with the fact that you will sometimes make mistakes, you will get it wrong, and you can't blame anyone else for that; but you can't let that stop you from taking the next big decision."

As we mentioned in the Introduction, in our work with executives, even those at very senior levels, we encounter individuals who do not see themselves as leaders. They have imagined leadership to be a very special skill or a "natural-born" ability they associate with prominent people in history. They allow this lack of confidence to hinder them from acting as leaders, especially in difficult situations. This can become a self-fulfilling prophecy; after all, if you don't believe in your ideas, why would anyone else? These clients tend to invest too much time worrying about what others think of them. It helps to remind them of the old saying: "You wouldn't worry so much about what people thought of you if you realized how seldom they did."

Managing Anxiety

Anxiety has an unnecessarily bad reputation and is often misunderstood. There are situations in life that naturally make you more anxious than others—sitting in the dentist's waiting area or meeting your future in-laws for the first time, for example. Your perception of a given scenario also affects your level of anxiety. Some people are filled with dread at the idea of giving a keynote speech at their company's sales conference, whereas others find the same prospect exciting and motivating.

Another component of anxiety is the *contagion* or *ripple effect*; that is, you pick up on others' emotions, which influence your own.[1] This is the case for both good and bad feelings. Think of how excitement ripples through a crowd at a concert, or how being in a roomful of nervous people can affect you. While we were writing this book, Colm took his son, Ian, to do his driving test. Looking around the room as he waited for the tester to call Ian, he noticed how the nervousness of the candidates spread like a virus.

Others can sense how you're feeling and can literally "catch" your anxiety. When they perceive you as nervous, they usually presume that you are lacking in confidence. It is a very short mental leap from seeing someone as lacking in confidence to assuming that he or she also lacks *competence*. Our own research with executives has uncovered a strong negative correlation between a person's level of anxiety and the extent to which a boss rates him or her as a leader. In short, the more anxious you appear, the less of "a leader" you'll seem to be.

Managing your level of anxiety is crucial for the moments we describe in this book. In order for you to effectively exercise leadership, you need to be able to *see yourself* as a leader. Your ability to see yourself as a leader is bound up with the image of yourself that you carry around in your head. Researchers have suggested that those who cannot include leadership, in some form, within their self-image may be missing a critical requirement for leadership development.[2] The U.S. Army has a much more succinct way of saying this: "You can't lead a cavalry charge if you think you look funny on a horse."

The most fundamental point is that there is **no link between anxiety and accuracy**. Just because you are nervous does not make your point or decision invalid. And the reverse is also true: just because the other people appear confident doesn't make their perspective valid. They may simply handle their anxiety better.

However, you *are* less likely to offer your opinion or to tell it like it is when you are nervous or anxious. Conor was the IT director of a manufacturing client of ours. He was brilliant in one-on-one meetings and was in fact deeply insightful about human behavior. He was also a star of large-scale company-wide communication forums and came across as a gifted and skilled presenter. However, Conor suffered real anxiety as a member of a leadership team with seven other executives. When he needed to make a point or intervene in a debate, he experienced butterflies in his stomach and shortness of breath. He sometimes spent so long getting himself ready to make his point that someone else got there before him.

We helped Conor manage his nerves, the first part of which was encouraging him to be honest with his colleagues about his occasional anxiety. He had a good relationship with everyone on the team; so once he explained what was going on, his colleagues made an effort to involve him more and helped him find less personally challenging ways to intervene.

The key point is to accept and manage your anxiety but also to be honest with others about the fact that you sometimes experience feelings of anxiety. In the Conclusion, when we will deal with creating emotional safety, we will talk more about the crucial role that the ability to be vulnerable plays in creating high-performance relationships.

As a child, and while being formally assessed for future careers, Henry was told that he should never pursue anything involving leadership or public speaking because of his chronic stutter. In recent years, he has begun to speak openly about the stuttering early in his client engagements, which makes him feel less anxious about it and ultimately causes him to stutter less.

When you are confronted with a difficult situation and you put off making a decision about it, you are setting up a potentially toxic spiral for your self-identity. Try to remember a time when you failed to confront an issue. You probably felt pretty bad about yourself; you may even have engaged in a little self-recrimination: "Why didn't I say something?" or "I should have called out that behavior." At some level, you know you should have done better. This can undermine your self-identity as a leader, which undermines your confidence and potentially makes it more likely that you will shrink from the next challenge.

Bear in mind that the other people involved in the situation—whether directly involved or merely observing—are also probably noticing that you didn't act, which will undermine your leadership capital in their eyes.

Believe it or not, being entirely free of anxiety isn't the answer; it's actually possible to be *too* emotionally stable. People with very low levels of anxiety can become arrogant and tend to be immune to feedback. There may have been an absence of what we call a *decent doubt*—that is, appropriate levels of anxiety—in the boardrooms of Enron, Tyco, Parmalat, and Anglo Irish Bank.

As martial arts practitioners, we've found that other martial arts fighters who are consistently successful are not simply supremely confident in their abilities. Those with a little anxiety about their ability tend to respect their opponent and always expect a hard contest. When they don't feel like training on dark winter mornings, they tend to ask themselves, "What if I don't train today but my opponent does?"

Anxiety can become the fuel that propels you to do better next time. But if you let it get out of hand, it will stop you from seeing yourself as a leader and therefore from acting as a leader.

Step Up

The leadership moments surrounding decisions involve making *and* communicating these decisions and managing the anxiety that may accompany them. The following suggestions will help you determine how to step up in each of these situations.

About Making Decisions

As we've noted, you often have to make a decision even when you don't have all the information you would like. Sometimes, you notice a behavior in your team that you should challenge. You can either grasp the opportunity as it arises or let it pass by. The more often you take action, the more confident you will become in doing so, and the easier it gets—provided you are consciously learning from those experiences. However, every time you fail to do something, you make it harder to step up to the plate for the next challenge.

Think of this ability and willingness to step up as a competency or skill that you can develop over time. With practice, you will get better at exercising decision leadership, and as you get better, you will find it easier and easier to recognize these moments and step up.

Use the Prioritization Filter

We use the Prioritization Filter (see Figure 3.1) as a tool with our executive clients to help them decide what they will and won't do. This approach encourages you to sort your tasks into

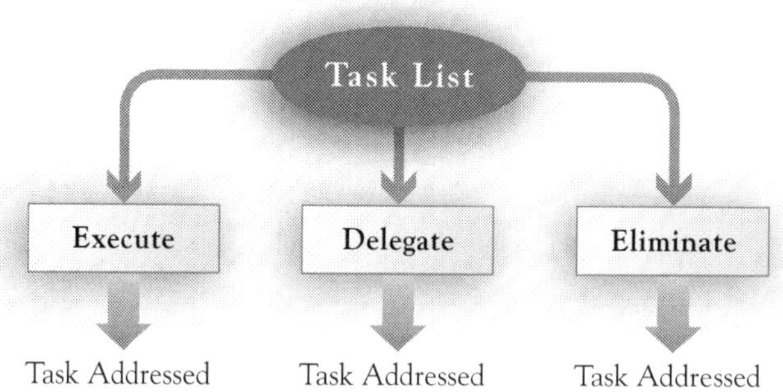

Figure 3.1 The Prioritization Filter
Copyright © Dynamic Results, LLC

one of three categories: those that you will **execute** (do yourself), **delegate** (give to someone else), or **eliminate** (not do at all). Sorting the tasks often involves making difficult decisions, especially the decision to eliminate a task—which can be particularly hard when you are having to eliminate a task that you enjoy but that ought to be gone from your agenda.

In a perfect world, people would never overcommit, and circumstances would never shift or change once they had a plan. In the real world, you no doubt struggle to keep all your commitments as they were originally stated. Many people have difficulty telling others that they won't do a task that others are expecting them to do, and we frequently observe our clients feeling overwhelmed by what they have committed to do within a given period of time. If you fail to complete something you've promised to do, you erode your credibility—and your leadership capital will take a big hit. It is best to come clean as soon as possible about the things you eliminate from your to-do list, even if it feels uncomfortable to do so.

Henry once heard someone say, "The idea that we will 'get it all done' is a fallacy. We won't get it all done, we aren't getting it all done now, and we will have a to-do list when we die." If you're confused about what to start putting on your Eliminate list, begin by simply acknowledging that you're not going to read the articles you've been "planning to read" for the last six months. Throw them out, delete them, burn them—do whatever you have to do. If you ever have the bandwidth and interest to read them someday, Google will have all the information you need at your fingertips.

Other things you may put on your Eliminate list could include conversations you're not willing to have (as proven by the fact that you have avoided them for a long time), chores you're not completing (cleaning out a garage), and even something like quitting smoking.

Henry coached the COO of a national distribution company. When the coaching began, the COO was overweight, smoking, experiencing marital problems, struggling in relationships with his children, and he was given six months to improve his relationships at work or be fired. When Henry conducted the initial interview as part of the coaching engagement, he asked the COO if he planned to address some of the health issues he had. The COO said, "My doctor told me that I have to lose weight and quit smoking, but I'm not willing to do those things right now; I've got too much stress."

Henry said, "OK," and instead asked the COO to do some homework between coaching sessions by researching the life expectancy of someone with his age, weight, and stress level who also smoked. In the next coaching session, the COO said, "A man my age, fifty-three, with my family's medical history, my weight, and so forth, can expect to live for another eight to ten years."

Because the client was not willing to "eliminate" smoking, Henry asked him to move smoking to the Execute category and proactively go to his daughters and wife, declaring his intention to die by January 27, 2017, as a result of being overweight and continuing to smoke. Before we were done reverse-engineering the process of funeral arrangements and financial planning, the client decided that he wasn't willing to have that conversation. Over the next two years, he quit smoking, took off more than fifty pounds, started exercising, and left to start his own company. Our point is that you must be intentional about categorizing your "intentions" into the three categories, and you always have the right to move them.

In some situations, we also encourage clients to sort their task list into Will Do, Might Do, and Won't Do categories. Will Do are the things to which you have already dedicated resources, such as time and funding. Might Do are things you have every intention of doing and to which you have not yet allocated resources. Won't Do items are the same as those on your Eliminate list.

Act on Your Top Priorities

We knew a man who was very good at listing his priorities from one through ten. However, he always busied himself with his lowest while other people were waiting for decisions about his top items. You can avoid that trap by using our Priority Quadrants tool (see Figure 3.2).

Here is how to use the tool:

1. Select a time frame—a week, a month, or whatever period of time you're likely to be overwhelmed.
2. Write your **top four priorities** during that time frame in the four boxes in the chart, in order of importance to you. You can have fewer and no more than four. We also challenge our clients not to collapse more than four into four.
3. Identify the next step to take for each of the four priorities. Write the steps in the space at the bottom of the appropriate box.
4. Enter a deadline for completion for each step.
5. When you have completed a step, enter the next step and a new deadline by modifying the electronic version of the tool. (At the end of this chapter, we've given you a link to download the document.)

You don't want to fall into the trap of working on your lowest priorities and forcing others to wait for decisions about the really important things. This tool will keep you from addressing priorities that are lower than the four in the chart until you have moved the ball as far downfield as you can for each of them.

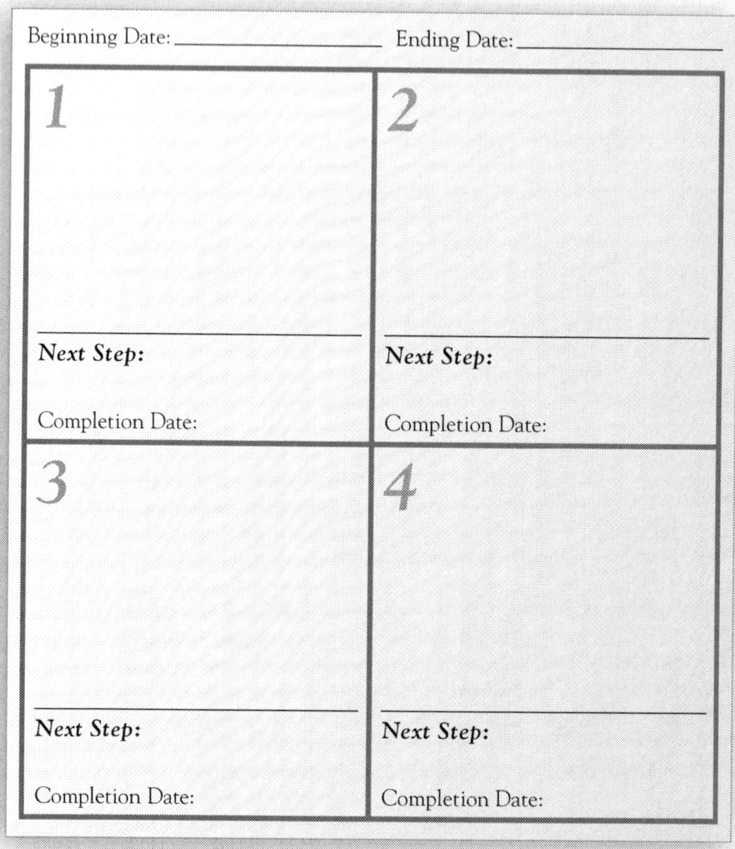

Figure 3.2 The Priority Quadrants Tool
Copyright © Dynamic Results, LLC

Decide or Decide to Not Decide . . . Don't Procrastinate

Here are a few more suggestions for improving your ability to be decisive when it matters.

1. **Look back over decisions you've made in the last ten days.** How timely were they? How clearly did you communicate

them? How transparent and accountable are you for these decisions? How clearly have you communicated them to key stakeholders? Can you identify any themes (lack of timeliness, lack of accountability, poor communication)? Even just heightening your awareness of the habitual issues with your decision making will make you focus on improving this aspect of your decision leadership.

2. **Decide *when to decide* and when not to.** The idea is not to turn yourself into an action junky, running around making decisions to demonstrate your decisiveness. There is absolutely a right time to hold off. We call this *systematic waiting* or *masterful inactivity*, and you engage in it by purposefully deciding that you are *not* going to decide or act. It doesn't mean drifting into inactivity or burying yourself in busywork to put off making a decision. It is also sometimes appropriate to recognize that a decision needs to be made, but that you are not the right person to make the decision. Sometimes you will want to make a decision yourself; other times, you will want to challenge a group to make a decision.

Although the tactic of masterful inactivity is often useful, we want to give you a serious health warning about this approach. By failing to intervene in a situation, you allow it to continue as it is or even escalate. Essentially, when you avoid discussing something that should be discussed because it is or will be a problem, you are passively endorsing whatever is happening. We advise our clients to be very careful of the signals they send when they choose not to decide or act.

A useful analogy is to imagine yourself at the foot of a large uncharted mountain. There are several paths up, but you can't tell which one is best. If the weather is bad, it is a smart decision to wait until it clears before you start your climb. This is systematic waiting. You know that a key variable in the situation will predictably change. However, if you just can't tell which path is right, no amount of standing at the bottom of the mountain and staring at it will help.

You will have to choose a path knowing that it might be the wrong one and that you may have to retrace your steps and try another one. At least you will have eliminated one possibility. With this said, if you are feeling emotionally charged about a person and want to do something drastic (for example, fire her, tell her off, or tell on her), you may do well to wait overnight, sleep on it, and see if you feel the same way in the morning.

3. **Know when to change your decision.** As economist J. M. Keynes said, "When the facts change, I change my opinions." As we know, human beings tend to want to stick by their ideas and opinions. So when we begin to suspect that we have made a bad decision, we *don't* often think about reversing it; instead, we actually become *more* committed to it. Colm reports that he displays this behavior quite often when driving. If he gets lost, he doesn't stop and ask for directions; rather, he tends to speed up! At those times, his wife often quotes Yogi Berra and says, "We're lost, but we're making good time."

This trap is represented in the saying, "Having lost sight of our goals, we redoubled our efforts!" That sounds like a good idea, until you really think about what you are actually doing. This often presents itself as the fallacy of the sunk-cost argument: "We have spent so much money on developing this product, we can't stop now." One of the most egregious examples of this was the Long Island Lighting Company's decision to build a nuclear power plant at Shoreham in the northeastern United States. The company spent $5 billion on a proposal that was originally budgeted to cost $75 million and that never generated a single kilowatt of electricity. They eventually abandoned the project altogether.

You should generally stick to your guns once you make a decision. But beware of becoming so emotionally attached to a decision that you're merely out to prove that you were right in the first place. If this is the case, it's time to make a different decision.

About Communicating Decisions

When Henry lived in Texas, he learned the expression "putting lipstick on a pig"—that is, describing something ugly as something attractive, like making a tough project sound easy while recruiting people to work on it. This may appear to be an easy strategy while you're using it, but you lose leadership credibility over the long term as people discover the real story. Think back to the Shackleton ad. He described the job of going out on an exploration as being very dangerous and potentially life threatening, so when the team members went to actually do it and they got stuck in the ice, he did not lose leadership credibility. His team still believed in him and acted accordingly.

Remember when communicating a decision that *what is simple is clear, and what is clear gets done*. You lose integrity every time you fail to honestly describe a tough situation as it really is. Putting lipstick on a pig is the enemy of clarity and simplicity; it undermines your chances of having others complete what you need them to.

To move a decision forward, you might try these steps:

1. **Recognize when an opportunity for a tough discussion exists, and *tell it like it is*.** For example, a manager who wants to sugarcoat a difficult situation might sound like this in a conversation with a direct report:

Manager: I hope you're having a great week. Listen, I need a competitive market analysis report on my desk tomorrow for a board meeting I have in the late afternoon. I know it sounds like a lot of work, but it really isn't if an expert like you handles it. Could you take care of it for me?

Report: I would like to help you, but I need to know what the report looks like.

Manager: I'm thinking that we should be able to show the market potential, along with our and our competitors' existing market penetration. We should break out this information by state for everything in the U.S. west of the Mississippi River. Again, it's a manageable request if you start now.

In this moment, both the direct report and manager are likely to recognize that the request is anything but easy. While the manager is trying to pose his request in a nonthreatening way, he is sacrificing leadership credibility in an attempt to have his employee perceive him as "nice." He wants to package the request in a palatable—but not entirely accurate—way. But that doesn't help anyone get a clear picture of what truly needs to be done.

We would suggest an alternative and more direct approach:

Manager: I hope you're having a great week. Listen, I've got a challenging request that may be difficult to meet. I need to pick an expert to take charge, and I'm coming to you. We need about three days' worth of work performed by 3 P.M. tomorrow, and accepting my request would almost certainly interrupt your life balance. We need a full competitive market analysis of the Western region. I'm seeing a ten-slide PowerPoint deck with no more than eight words per slide and a map image to represent the particular states you are reporting on. We will need information such as market potential and ours versus our competitors' market penetration broken out by state. Can you handle this and get us across the finish line?

The manager is building leadership credibility here. He's making it clear that the request will be a challenge, but also letting the direct report know that *he* is the expert being chosen for it. The employee is likely to appreciate the manager's honesty and that he is in tune with the effort required to get the job done.

2. **Maintain your integrity when change occurs.** Sometimes you will do a brilliant job of describing a tough situation and getting everyone on board with a plan—and then have the rug pulled out from under you. The people you interact with may even confuse a change in the environment with a change in your personal integrity, and wonder why "you said it would be this other way." A lot of people try to put a positive spin on changes by saying something like, "This isn't really a big change. It's just another way of looking at the same thing."

We worked with a client organization that had experienced double-digit growth for many decades. When the global recession hit them in 2008, they started eliminating benefits and profit distributions to keep the company profitable. They also were forced to reduce their staff from thirty-eight hundred to fewer than six hundred. The road of contraction was bumpy.

We suggested that they follow Machiavelli's advice: "When committing atrocities, commit them all at once." In other words, look out a year in advance and make any cuts you believe you will have to make *all at once and now*. This course of action would be fiscally intelligent and, perhaps more important, more humane for the people you plan to keep. You would spare them rounds of painful layoffs.

The client didn't follow our advice. With each successive layoff or cut in benefits, the leadership team delivered messages like, "It's not really a cut in benefits; it's more like a reallocation," and "I know we said there wouldn't be any more layoffs, and the ones we did this week aren't really 'more'; they're just helping us reach the higher end of the worst-case scenario projections we shared with you six months ago." The employee engagement surveys we administered for this organization demonstrated what you probably realize intuitively: every time the leadership team delivered such a message, and even though they may have actually believed the message, they lost credibility.

We've also seen this (and other) client organizations handle the same type of ugly, nasty, uncomfortable situation—but in a way that demonstrated high leadership credibility. They conveyed information as follows: "Six months ago, we told you that we didn't believe we would have additional layoffs. While we believed that to be true at the time, we realize now that we were wrong. Things have not gone as well as we thought they would, and as a result, we need to lay off another two hundred people."

In this second scenario, leadership honestly admitted to a mistake—which preserved some measure of its credibility with employees.

About Managing Anxiety

You can better manage your emotional reactions, such as anxiety, by understanding the connections between your physiology (how your body acts), your cognition (what and how you think), and your emotions (how you feel).

Because all three elements are connected, you can intervene in any one of them in order to affect the other levels. Essentially, you can *act* your way into a new approach to thinking and feeling, *feel* your way into a new approach to acting and thinking, or *think* your way into a new approach to feeling and acting. Table 3.1 demonstrates how intervening in any one of the three areas—acting, feeling, or thinking—creates a new approach in the other two.

People who struggle with anxiety can usually deal with their nerves successfully when they can control their physical reactions. They are then able to appear confident to others who in turn become more willing to listen and pay attention to what they have to say.

When you are nervous, the principal physical symptom has to do with your breathing. You tend to take shallow breaths, get short of breath, breathe from your chest rather than your diaphragm, and talk faster. You may start to yawn; your voice loses its timbre, and you find yourself using the high-pitched squeaky voice that is a dead giveaway of your anxiety level. Getting in control of your breathing is the key to regaining confidence and to appearing confident. The following are two tips for doing so:

- Concentrate on **deliberately slowing down your breathing** and ensure that you are taking full, deep breaths. Place your hand on your belly and feel your belly rise and fall with each breath. You can visualize your breath coming in and going out through your heart.
- Use a rhythm: breathe in for a count of three, then hold your breath for a count of three. Then breathe out for a count of three, followed again by a hold for a count of three. Do this at least three times.

These techniques have the great advantage that they are unobtrusive. You can use them during a meeting and nobody will notice—until you speak up confidently! You also experience the

Table 3.1 Thinking: Feeling: Action Strategy

Cognitive Strategy	Effect on Behavior	Effect on Feeling
Reframe the issue—for example, choose to see the exit of a valued employee as an opportunity for her and allow for the possibility that she might return later with better skills, rather than focusing on the short-term impact on your business.	You move from ignoring, shunning, or punishing the employee to facilitating a graceful exit.	You move from feeling sorry for yourself and angry at her to feeling pleased for her.
Behavioral Strategy	**Effect on Thinking**	**Effect on Feeling**
Engage in any form of physical activity—for example, getting up and going for a walk when you are stuck on a problem.	The physical act of moving forward frees up the psychological drive to move forward.	Physical exercise, especially outside in fresh air, creates endorphin flow that generates positive feelings.
Emotional Strategy	**Effect on Thinking**	**Effect on Behavior**
Engage in a mood-enhancing activity—for example, listening to music that you know puts you in a particular mood.	The music creates the emotional background that is conducive to a particular type of thinking (as we discussed in relation to the Mood and Cognition Model; see Figure 1.2).	Depending on the music you choose, you create the physical urge to slow down or speed up.

psychological advantage of feeling in control of *something*, even if it is only your own breathing.

In addition to managing your physiology, you can adopt either a cognitive or an emotional approach by

- Seeing the situation from another perspective
- Thinking through the worst that could happen and identifying how you would handle that
- Helping yourself feel differently about the situation

The last of those techniques is based on the idea of *grounding* or *anchoring*, which requires that you spend time imagining and connecting to a positive image of yourself—a time when you were at your best. You need to create a real, visceral memory of that experience. Then when you are getting nervous, you can call upon this memory to get back the feeling of a confident you. This requires real work; it's not just daydreaming about the good times, but creating a strong, emotionally compelling memory that you can connect to under pressure.

Colm used this approach when he started playing golf. His short game and putting were average, but his driving was erratic. The greater the number of people who were watching him hit a drive, the worse his nerves became, and his driving suffered. He started to practice the driver swing during gym sessions and listened to the same song on his iPod for that part of the workout. Whenever he was waiting on the tee for his turn to hit the drive, he would quietly (mercifully) sing the song to himself. This helped calm his nerves, as he associated that song with a fluid swing. He has not become a good golfer, but he no longer blames his nerves—just a complete absence of natural talent!

Many people don't *have* to struggle with anxiety often, but as we mentioned earlier, a complete absence of it isn't always a good sign either. If you *never* experience anxiety, you may not be taking appropriate risks; you may be keeping yourself locked safely inside your comfort zone. If you wish to know where a healthy dose of anxiety may be missing in your life, try answering the following questions:

- Who is anxious about something that you are not anxious about?
- What is it that he is anxious about? What is he afraid might happen?
- What if he's right?

Summary of Key Learnings in Chapter Three

- Leaders rarely have perfect information. However, they are able to decide on a course of action, commit to it, and communicate their decision confidently and convincingly.
- Your ability to decide is undermined when you don't realize how often you do fail to face problems, when you want to be and be seen as a nice person, and when you doubt your own ability to decide and lead.
- There is no link between anxiety and accuracy. Being anxious about your point does not mean that it is not valid or worthwhile. Likewise, do not presume that those who express their ideas confidently are more competent than they really are.
- You can act your way into a new way of thinking and feeling, feel your way into a new way of acting and thinking, or think your way into a new way of feeling and acting.
- Control of your breathing is the key to regaining confidence and to appearing confident.
- Knowing and acting on your priorities—along with your ability to determine what you will do, what you will delegate,

and what you will eliminate from your agenda—are all critical to your ability to lead.

Your Next Steps to Step Up and Become More Decisive

- Consider a current project or decision, identify the top five considerations your team must take into account, and weight-rank them. When you have reconciled four of the five, you have at least 80 percent of the information you need to make a decision.
- Examine a key project that you are running right now. Are you waiting for perfection to act on something? Are you or other team members trying to analyze your way into the future? Identify at least one key decision that you need to make and really challenge yourself to figure out what's stopping you from taking an intelligent risk.
- Identify an upcoming opportunity in your organization to be honest and tell it like it is (assigning a tough project, giving difficult news, and so on). What can you do to make this happen or to encourage your team to take this approach?
- Identify an impending interaction in which you will probably feel some anxiety. Commit to trying one of the approaches discussed (physiological, cognitive, or emotional) and notice how it works for you. Help others who suffer this anxiety to do the same.
- Use the Prioritization Filter to help manage your to-do list.
- Use the Priority Quadrants tool for at least two weeks and whenever you feel overwhelmed.
- Identify a current situation in which you have decided not to decide. Make a list of all the people who need to know this, and make a point of ensuring that you communicate it to them within the next three business days.

Step Up Link

Priority Quadrants Tool

CHAPTER FOUR

Act When You Are the Problem

Imagination is more important than knowledge.
—Albert Einstein

Our Promise

Many potential leadership moments present themselves during times of organizational change. This chapter will explain the forces that require today's companies to change and those that inhibit you and others from changing. It will provide techniques for you to make real changes in yourself, which is the essential first step to leading change in others.

Recognize the Moment

Moments of leadership arise when the people around you are stuck in old ways of thinking and behaving. However, catalyzing change in others requires that you are comfortable with changing yourself.

We can all agree that we are living in an age of unprecedented change. Although it is tempting to hope that the turbulence will settle down at some point, few organizational scholars or operating managers believe this to be true. We may not know what the new environment will look like, but we are pretty sure it won't resemble the past, and we can say that it is very likely to be characterized by continued rapid change.

Today's organizations have a real problem in terms of generating sustainable growth and earnings. In the past, the holy grail of strategy was to identify and protect a source of sustainable competitive advantage—to exploit a competency that gave you an advantage against your competition. Organizations hoped to identify unique competencies that were rare, valuable, and difficult or costly to imitate. For example, Kodak's preeminence in photographic reproduction was one such advantage.

That approach is no longer tenable. Companies can no longer seek to exploit their current advantages or leverage their existing skill sets. New competencies and capabilities are emerging all the time, and the time frame within which you can benefit from any advantage thus gained is becoming shorter and shorter. For example, we developed an assessment process we call the Leadership Edge™ to measure the competencies critical to twenty-first-century leadership. It includes such elements as cross-cultural sensitivity, which was not on anybody's list of competencies not too many years ago. Traditionally, many teams were culturally homogenous—something else that's becoming increasingly rare. Accountability was also easier to drive back when people wanted to stay with a company for twenty years and collect a pension; however, that's not the case these days, when they plan to leave an organization in three or four years. As experts in the field of talent assessment, we have to be very aware that the competencies we assess and indeed our own ability to assess them need to be continually challenged and updated.

Organizational researchers such as Peter Senge have claimed that the key to future success will depend on a company's ability to out-innovate its competition—which is based on its ability to out-learn its competition.[1] This means that organizations which learn faster than their competitors will succeed in the new environment. Those who get stuck in outmoded ways of thinking will not even survive.[2] And of course, **organizations that must learn faster require people who learn faster**, who are not stuck in obsolete thinking and approaches.

Unfortunately, history has shown that the more successful you are—both as an organization and as an individual—the more difficult the transition may be. A phenomenon we call the *trap of success* dictates that both companies and people start to believe in their success recipe. After a period of struggle and adaptation, they assume they've figured out how to be successful in their industry. And the more successful they become, the more they emotionally invest in their success recipe—especially those senior leaders who may have been responsible for crafting and codifying the recipe.

An organization that thinks this way sounds like this: "We have a seventy-year history of serving our customers, and we know how it's done." Perhaps there is not a more glaring example of this type of thinking than Kodak, which we cited earlier. It is sad to note that Kodak had in fact patented digital photography technology before any other company, but failed to exploit this because of excessive reliance on its existing business model. On the individual level, this attitude sounds more like, "I've been doing this for ten years; I'm sure I know what I'm doing."

This kind of thinking can render an organization **learning disabled**; that is, the organization stops actively seeking to learn new things and attempts instead to exploit existing learning. If you are one of the senior leaders in your organization, ask yourself if you are at risk of investing in your past success recipe and failing to be a thought leader. If you are in a reasonably fast-moving industry, ask yourself whether you are launching products that actively cannibalize your "star" products. If you aren't, you are risking having your competitors do this for you.

Let's take a couple of computer industry examples of companies that have embraced change and of some that have resisted it. One of our clients was the CEO of a boutique software business that offered an in-demand and unique technology. After struggling in their early years, the business was doing so well that they had huge difficulty keeping up with demand. The CEO often talked about how stressed he was trying to find suitably qualified software engineers to meet the demand for his product.

In his mind, the key to success was having good engineers to deliver software solutions, because that was how he had built the business. However, we realized as outsiders that he did not have a recruitment issue. He had a pricing issue—specifically, that prices were too low. Although he lost some potential customers when he increased his prices, they were the least profitable ones. And he was able to slim down his back-order book to a size that he could deal with by deploying the resources he had. He changed his mind-set from looking to grow the business to looking to optimize its profitability. His company may never get to be the next Microsoft; but he now serves his client base exceptionally well, is rewarded for his efforts, and is a much healthier, happier, and less stressed individual.

Microsoft has given us a great example of hubris in its commitment to an outmoded success recipe. Following in Bill Gates's footsteps, Steve Ballmer remained committed to desktop-based systems controlled by complex user interfaces and operating systems. Meanwhile, the rest of the industry recognized that consumers were moving from desktop to mobile devices. Ballmer insisted on ignoring the rapid move away from Microsoft legacy products (desktop) to upstart (mobile) products. He also ignored the industry's move to cloud-based computing—and ended up jumping in too late. He made the same error with browsers, introducing the failed Bing search engine. And while Apple and other companies looked to integrate their offerings into social media, Ballmer and Microsoft ignored the trend until it may have been too late. In the end, the only information that may have led Ballmer to act quickly followed the disastrous introduction of Windows 8 to the marketplace, when he decided to step down as CEO. In the first week of Ballmer's announcement of his resignation, Microsoft stock shot way up (a great thing for Balmer's personal net worth).

IBM is another computer industry case of an organization that stuck to a recipe for too long. It has since managed to transform itself into a service and consulting business, but the transformation was quite traumatic. The company's loyalty to the old way almost caused its downfall. The attitude of Dell Computers suggests that the computer industry may have learned this lesson. It is interesting to note that in interviews, Michael Dell takes particular exception to interviewers referring to the "Dell Way," a term that he apparently resists for fear of the company's existing model hardening into the type of dogma that creates the trap of success.[3]

As you figure out your own challenges and develop the optimal approach for your organization, remember that there are no best practices or success recipes. There are only *next* practices: your current best thinking, which is subject to continuous challenge and stretch.

Good managers naturally want to get out in front of and proactively manage the changes required by the developing "new normal." Unfortunately, many people view change as something that *they do to others*, failing to see their own necessary role in it. The term "organizational change" is something of an oxymoron, as organizations don't change until the people in them do. Genuine transformation and the ability to continually learn and adapt only come when people open up to the possibility that they themselves will need to alter their attitudes, beliefs, and behaviors—just like the CEO of the software firm we referred to earlier.

It's not easy for most people to accept the possibility that some of their most cherished and entrenched beliefs about how the world works may be wrong. All of us like to see ourselves as capable, competent, and—as we've discussed—right most of the time. When you acknowledge that a valued belief may be wrong or misguided, your view of yourself as competent is challenged. What ensues is a feeling of discomfort that results from holding two conflicting beliefs (that you are a smart person and that one of your strongly held beliefs is wrong)—a feeling that everyone tries to avoid. There are two ways that people try to protect themselves from this feeling, and we'll look at these in the next sections.

Mental Models

The first way is a result of there being too much information in the environment to fully process. Because we can pay attention only to a tiny part of it, we develop mental models—that is, rules of thumb that we use to simplify and make sense of the world. We tend to pick out salient features in any situation and fill in the rest from our memory. Have you ever found yourself halfway home without realizing how you got there? Your memory was taking care of the driving and the directions while your mind was distracted elsewhere. You were literally on autopilot! Your mental models determine the boundaries of your rationality. "Thinking outside the box" is actually not possible for a human being. You can think inside a different box or a bigger box, but there's always a box—and its walls represent the limits of the mental model you use to make sense of a given situation.

Real learning occurs when you can *recognize* the mental models you are using and challenge their validity, and when you can see the walls of the box for what they are: artificial boundaries on your thinking.

Ken Starkey, professor of management and organizational learning at Nottingham University in the United Kingdom and an expert on leadership development, writes that the ability to challenge our own thoughts, feelings, values, attitudes, beliefs, and habits of mind (that is, our mental models) is a key element of developing the ability to exercise leadership.[4]

Take the example of one of our clients. He hired us to help him achieve the role of president of one division in a rapidly growing software company. He excelled and became the highest-performing president of seven divisions in this company. He saw the company grow and prosper, and even had his image plastered on the NASDAQ screen in Times Square. He did so well that he was promoted and had two divisions under him.

He complained during executive coaching sessions with Henry that his CEO was "always" dismissing his ideas and "putting him down" in meetings with other executives. This was the mental model he had created to explain the situation. He began to dislike the CEO and spoke about going somewhere else where his ideas would be respected.

As his coach, Henry found his claims that his CEO "always shot down his ideas" to be incongruent with a three-year history of promotions and bonuses—so Henry challenged his thinking, in effect to expose the mental model his client was using. The following is a summarized version of the coaching dialogue:

Client: My CEO hates all of my ideas, is always critical of me, and does not respect me.

Henry: That sounds like a tough environment to operate in.

Client: It is. It's hard to keep innovating when all of your ideas are being dismissed and your boss isn't interested in hearing your thoughts.

Henry: You are closer to the work and to the relationship with your CEO than I am, and I know that I may be missing a lot of context for the discussion we're having. Still, I wonder, what other explanations may be possible for your CEO challenging you in the way he does?

Client: I get it. This is the part of the coaching discussion where you ask me to consider options other than the ones I'm currently considering. It's the old paradigm switcheroo, right?

Henry: Right. I am asking you to **remain curious** for a moment. Just for the purposes of our discussion, what else might be happening during the interactions you are having with your boss?

Client: Well, I've been doing this long enough with you that I think you want me to say that my boss is challenging me for the purpose of continuing to develop me as an executive. It's all for my own good, and I should take my medicine, right?

Henry: As I said, I don't know what your boss's motivations are. I do know that he's promoted you twice in the last two years, seeks your advice on big decisions outside the realm of your core responsibilities, and keeps pulling you into meetings in which, at least on paper, you don't have a formal role. I realize that you think he doesn't like you and does not respect you, and I'm struggling to understand why he would do all that if your assessment of his feelings is accurate. We have two ideas on the table. One is that your boss doesn't like or respect you, and the other is that your boss challenges your ideas in a way that you feel is . . . well, challenging. My question is this: Which story does the evidence at hand best support?

Client: You know, I may not like the way he speaks to me in meetings, his tone and delivery and all that. But he certainly behaves like someone who wants me to continue to move up and have more impact in the organization.

Henry: What if your homework was to look during your next few interactions for evidence of his *confidence* in you? How would it affect your behavior if you knew when going into meetings that you had his full confidence—and that he would like to continue to see you prove your ideas?

Our client did his homework, challenging his mental model that the CEO did not trust or value him. He then began to renegotiate the style of communication his CEO had with him, while at the same time moving forward with confidence knowing that the CEO trusted and believed in him. At the time of this writing, he received a third and much bigger promotion. He is now influencing the entire organization.

This example demonstrates how important it is for you to have your thinking questioned, so that you can examine your own mental models. Take a moment now to think of the times when someone's reaction surprised you. What assumptions had you been making about the person? Why was the person's action so surprising? If you can identify three or four examples, you may even be able to spot some themes. For example, do you sometimes assume that people feel guilt when they actually feel shame or embarrassment? (People who feel guilty are motivated to repair their error; people who feel ashamed just feel bad about it.)

The following story about a company ignoring basic science is an example of the power of making your mental models explicit.

In the early 1970s, International Distillers and Vintners were looking to create new alcoholic beverages to expand their portfolio. They had a subsidiary in Ireland called Gilbeys and challenged the management to suggest drinks that would leverage the company's Irish heritage. The management thought about the two strengths that Ireland had at the time, whiskey and dairy. Could they combine these two?

There was a fundamental problem: milk and cream are oil-based liquids, and whiskey is water based. As any high school science student knows, oil and water don't mix, so a drink made of cream and whiskey was not physically possible. This accepted way of thinking held great sway in the technical community. However, it was only by challenging this fundamental assumption that the idea of a cream liqueur was created. Somewhere, somehow, someone in the company saw a potential leadership moment and decided to test the assumption.

The truth is that oil and water don't mix *easily*, which is different from not being able to mix at all. Once people accepted this new way of thinking, creating this cream liqueur became merely a processing challenge. The Bailey's Irish Cream brand was successfully launched and became one of the most valuable beverage alcohol brands in the world.

The example shows the importance of having your fundamental assumptions and beliefs challenged rigorously and regularly. This is especially true for successful organizations where the success recipe—the way to make money in an industry—may have hardened into dogma such as "oil and water don't mix." Such an assumption leaves you vulnerable to competitors who think outside your company's particular box. Because your company's box is a composite of its people's boxes, it is the people's boxes that need to expand.

Another company that made its mental model explicit was the KAO Corporation, a cosmetics firm that had a hugely successful business in Japan. Most of its earnings came from a single product, as Japanese women at one time wanted to create a perfectly white, smooth visage regardless of their natural skin type. KAO had the market-leading brand in this segment. In the 1980s, as fashion changed and the look became less fashionable, KAO faced a huge challenge to its business. As it lost its traditional customer base, it faced increasingly tough competition from both Japanese and international brands.

A real breakthrough came when KAO challenged how they were **defining the problem**. If the problem remained "how to compete in the cosmetics industry," KAO had a bleak future. However, someone or some group of people in the company thought about the assumptions they were making about the nature of their industry—and even the nature of what they did. The end result was a decision that they were not a cosmetics company, but had real competence in "surface coating technology." They redefined the question about the problem as, "In what environment would being great at surface coating technology be an advantage?" They identified the manufacture of floppy disks as a potential industry and went on to succeed in that area.

Although both of the stories above demonstrate the power of a company challenging its assumptions, both results were realized because at least one person in each company stepped up during a leadership moment.

Cognitive Biases

As we saw earlier, one problem in our perception of reality is that we don't take in all of the available data in forming our impressions. The second feature of our mental makeup that protects us from experiencing two conflicting feelings is called *cognitive bias*. This simply means that we are highly selective about what information we *choose* to focus on. We opt for data that confirm our mental models, and we ignore or dismiss data that challenge them.

One MIT researcher has estimated that we process only one-trillionth of the information available to us.[5] We establish and reinforce a simplified model of the world around us, a model that operates without our conscious awareness, and it takes effort to be open to new possibilities that challenge this model.

Harvard professor Michael Roberto examined the climbing disaster on Mount Everest in 1996 as an illustration of how cognitive biases can impair decision making and problem solving. Five of the eight-person climbing party, including experienced guides Bob Hall and Scott Fischer, lost their lives on Everest, having failed to successfully descend the mountain.

Roberto contends that several cognitive biases were in play and contributed to errors of judgment on the fateful day. One type of bias was the failure to ignore sunk costs. In other words, the climbers felt that because they'd come so far, they had to keep going. They passed the point where they had to turn back to ensure a safe descent and felt that they couldn't abandon their quest for the summit. Errors of this nature occur all the time in business; clients often refuse to cancel a project because of the time and effort they've already put into it. However, contrary to common practice, the only rational bases for deciding to persevere with a project are future cost and future benefit.

The second issue that Roberto identified is *overconfidence bias*, which is the tendency for people to overestimate their ability to deliver. Fischer and Hall thought they had cracked the code to Everest and could get any reasonably fit person to the summit and back down safely. We saw a number of clear examples of overconfidence bias in the 1990s when several Western fast-moving consumer goods brands entered China trying to deploy their existing business model. Most organizations failed miserably early on and had to radically change their approach in order to be successful in that market. A business school professor we knew said that the only investment banker who profited from China in the 1990s was the one who missed the plane—meaning that every banker who invested in China lost money!

The third issue Roberto identified is *recency bias*, which is the tendency to overvalue recent events. The past three summers had been mild on the mountain, causing people to forget just how brutal the weather on Everest could be. We often see clients failing to learn the lessons of the past by thinking that the recent past is a better predictor of the future than the medium- or long-term past. Look at your sales projections now and challenge yourself as to whether you are using your best-ever quarter as the basis of your forecasts going forward. Even though there may be sensible reasons to believe that this is the case, be aware of your tendency to overestimate the relevance of recent events. Give the medium-term past a second look, just in case.[6]

• • •

Openness to change is a basic personality characteristic,[7] and although challenging mental models and cognitive biases is an effort for all of us, those who are lower on the openness-to-change scale will find doing so especially daunting. People who are highly open to change are intellectually curious and are great at starting new projects. They tend to have lots of varied interests, read a number of books at any one time, and enjoy interacting with all sorts of people. Those who are lower on the openness scale tend to like routine; although they don't like change, they're good at completing tasks (for example, they read one book at a time). The next time you go to a meeting, notice the people who always sit in the same place; this is a fairly reliable sign of low openness to change. Are you surprised to note who these people are? Are you one of them?

Step Up

Your leadership moments involve both those in which you must change and those in which you can facilitate change in others. Becoming more open to change requires that you recognize and challenge your own mental models—and learn from mistakes.

Recognize Your Mental Models

A client of ours misread the level of support she had for a proposal and was surprised when the board rejected it. She *could* simply recognize her mistake and learn to check more thoroughly for support before she presents her proposal in a board meeting. This would prompt her to change her behavior for future proposals, which in itself is of course worthwhile.

However, our client could have benefited more from going a bit deeper into her learning experience. This would involve challenging herself to understand how she forms assumptions about who supports her and who doesn't.[8] This would have prompted her to question her assumptions and beliefs about people and their allegiances and preferences, and to examine the signs and cues she missed or misread, which led to failing to gain support for her proposal.

Toyota developed a question-asking technique called the 5 Whys to explore the underlying causes of technical problems, a useful tool when attempting to expose hidden assumptions and beliefs. The technique involves asking "Why" five times to uncover a root cause and can be applied equally well to personal challenges or problems. It is vital when questioning your own performance that you approach the task from a position of curiosity rather than judgment. Our client's 5 Why process might look something like this:

"I didn't get enough support from the board."

"Why?"

"Because I didn't explicitly ask for it enough."

"Why?"

"Because I thought I already had enough support."

"Why?"

"Because I thought one board member would support it since she was positive and encouraging when I presented it to her before the meeting."

"Why?"

"Because that board member's validation is very important to me, and I read too much into her signs of encouragement."

"Why?"

"Because I need to be seen as competent, and that leads to mistaking signs of encouragement as signs of support."

As she reflects more deeply, it is really important that she maintain a perspective of *unconditional positive regard*, a phrase first coined by psychologist Carl Rogers.[9] In other words, she must resist blaming the board member who encouraged her and focus instead on *her own contribution* to the misunderstanding—as that is the only thing she can change. As she reflects in a compassionate way on her own performance, she comes to understand parts of her own makeup that contributed to the situation. True learning and change occur when she recognizes her need to be seen as competent and starts to deal with the ways in which that need creates problems. That is when she can change herself, not just her behavior.

We also see problems ensue when clients don't receive bad news soon enough, which allows them to persist with a flawed mental model. We often have clients say that their people are not assertive or clear enough in making suggestions or bringing attention to unpleasant events or circumstances. A variation on this theme arises when your team goes through a protracted explanation of their process before risking telling you their recommendation.

We recently sat through one of our client's management team meetings involving a discussion about which retail outlets to invest in and which to close. The CEO had a history of taking bad news badly, but had really been working on this aspect of his behavior. After almost two hours of explaining the methodology and detailing the financial rationale, the team finally presented their findings, eventually getting to what they felt was the contentious decision to shut down a store close to the organization's headquarters. To their surprise, the CEO was very receptive to the idea. He said that his intuition suggested that the store be closed, but he'd wanted to see what the team would recommend. The CEO displayed great listening behavior, was very encouraging and empathic during the presentation, and was somewhat surprised to hear us describe the conversation as "redundant." We explained that if he had been clearer about his intuition, the team would have avoided wasting not only the two hours getting to the recommendation but also the countless hours they presumably spent in getting the analysis *exactly right.*

The CEO was surprised when he saw how his behavior caused people to avoid giving him news that they thought he didn't want to hear. If you are generally the last to hear when a major problem has occurred, or if people go out of their way *not* to bring you bad news, ask yourself, "What is it about me and the way I react that causes people to feel that they need to tread lightly around me?" When you start to make changes in your own behavior, you will start to exercise real leadership in the moments that matter. We will say more about this in the Conclusion, when we deal with the subject of being the Director of Emotional Safety.

Get Assessed

Being genuinely curious about others' observations and feedback is the most crucial way to make personal change. Other people base how they deal with you on what they think about you, not on how *you believe* they should think about you. Receiving 360-degree feedback is most useful in understanding others' perspectives. It includes direct feedback from subordinates, peers, supervisors, and others, as well as a self-evaluation. This process gives you an opportunity to learn how others see you. A good coach or development partner can assist you in understanding how those perspectives help and hinder you on a daily basis.

We've found in our work with executive clients that most leaders rate themselves dramatically higher or lower than others rate them; very few of them accurately self-assess. One executive rated himself far better than his peers, boss, direct reports, and others rated him. Being this out of touch with how other people perceived him was costing him dearly. Our job as his coaches was to help him change behaviors to increase ratings from others while concurrently learning to accept that their perceptions were not shaped by his self-assessment. This executive went through his work life assuming that people liked his ideas better than they actually did, and liked *him* better than they actually did. He assumed that when other people were silent, they were passively agreeing with what he was saying. But his

360-degree feedback showed the truth: people were afraid and unwilling to deal with his reaction to constructive criticism.

Other executives tend to rate themselves much lower than do their rater groups. Overly self-critical people like this tend to drag others through unnecessary and redundant assessments of ideas. They're also unwilling to make necessary decisions in a timely way because they lack confidence. As it is with the "self-overraters," our job with these individuals is to close the gap between how our clients perceive themselves and how others perceive them to provide a more accurate view of how they operate in the real world.

Once you have solicited feedback from people in your circle, don't just ignore it; *declare* what you will work on. A former colleague of Henry's named Pat Hyndman, who coached CEOs for over fifty years, once said, "If one person in your circle calls you an ass, you may ignore that feedback. If two people in your circle call you an ass, you should get curious and examine the feedback. Look for truth in it. If three or more people in your circle call you an ass, buy a cart; you're an ass."

One of the most useful things we recommend a client do after receiving her assessment is to go back to her raters and say something along the lines of, "Thank you for providing me with feedback. After listening to what everyone had to say, here is what I've decided to work on. Please feel free to tell me when you see me falling back in these areas; also tell me when you see me doing well." Please note that we don't recommend that you explore any particular aspect of your assessment with a specific person. This usually comes across as some form of interrogation and breaks down trust.

Ask the "Magic Wand" Question

The magic wand question is, "If you could magically and permanently change one thing about me for the better, what would it be, and why?" If you start by asking that about yourself, you create emotional safety with others; maybe down the road they will invite you to give the same kind of feedback. We will talk more about emotional safety in the Conclusion.

To encourage our coaching clients to broach this topic, we ask them, "What is some feedback, right or wrong, that people have been consistently giving you that you may have been ignoring or refusing to listen to?"

You might also ask the magic wand question about your organization, by saying, "I know we've got a great thirty-year legacy of doing what we do really well. But what might our clients, suppliers, and shareholders change about us permanently and instantly if they had the power—even if they were wrong?"

We've seen outstanding and unexpected results come out of this sort of questioning on both the individual and the organizational level. These questions can be a catalyst for recognizing patterns in feedback you've received, making it harder to dismiss the feedback incidentally. In one case, a coaching client of ours realized that whereas his peers and direct reports used to perceive him as a "good listener," times had changed—and he needed to do more work to regain this reputation.

Pay Attention to What You Ignore

A variation on the magic wand question involves paying attention to feedback—from your suppliers, customers, employees, board of directors, or competitors—that your organization has received and hasn't taken seriously. This technique requires that you take a good look at what you might need to change, either as an organization or as individuals.

Have you or your company received feedback you don't like—and perhaps believe to be wrong? Henry was once part of a group of eight people who agreed that they would deliver material in front of one another; then each of them would receive feedback from the other seven. All they were allowed to say to the feedback was "Thank you"; they were not to debate it in any way, shape, or form.

Seven of the eight did just say, "Thank you." However, one person debated the feedback violently, and afterwards said to Henry, "You know, I really resent that I had to sit there and take this feedback from everyone."

Henry replied, "Well, we had an agreement that that's what we would do. Seven of us kept it, and you didn't."

And the person said, "Well, I would have accepted it if any of the feedback had been right, but it was all wrong."

Don't be that person. Instead ask yourself, "What if I am wrong about the feedback being wrong? What might I be missing?" You might also refer back to Pat Hyndman's words and "get curious."

Read More Than One Book at a Time

Formerly, Henry was a member of a CEO think tank. Each month, the group spent mornings listening to a subject-matter expert espouse a theory and tell the participants how they might be able to apply it in their businesses. During the afternoons, the group would unpack how they could apply the new ideas in their respective businesses. Finally, they would discuss their individual business challenges, for the purpose of drawing upon the group's collective wisdom and insight.

One speaker recommended reading more than one book at a time. He felt that this would help feed the brain in a way that was consistent with the environment in which the participants operated. All of them worked in positions where they received a lot of information on varied topics rapidly and, in some cases, at the same time.

Henry was staunchly opposed to the idea of multitasking. His approach was to put his full attention into whatever he was doing at the moment. He called it "single-tasking." Further, he was a traveling CEO and prided himself on using only carry-on bags, making it difficult to carry more than one book while on the road. He also doubted his own intellectual capacity for changing topics quickly.

Then he noticed how he watched television. He often channel-surfed back and forth between shows of vastly different genres and with very different content. He would switch as his interests changed. He soon realized that he could indeed do the same thing with books, training himself to function more effectively in an environment where he received a lot of information on varied topics rapidly and sometimes simultaneously.

We recommend that you leverage the electronic book format and not only read more than one book at a time but read from different genres and on different topics. At any given time, Henry now might be reading a book on spirituality, a business book, a biography, something on science, and a junk novel. Sometimes, he reads books written by people with opposing views on subjects such as politics. This keeps him engaged, interested, and open to new ideas. At a minimum, it helps him understand the opposing views better without dismissing them in an information vacuum.

Understand Someone You Don't Understand

As we discussed in Chapter Two, people tend to surround themselves with others who think as they do and agree with them. This kind of environment doesn't do much to support growth. You need people who think differently than you do in your life—both in and out of work. The best thing you can do is find the smartest person you know who often disagrees with you and seek understanding with that person.

When coaching our clients, they often complain about people who frequently disagree with them and with their ideas. We usually advise them to appreciate those people even if only for the fact that they give them a developmental opportunity that like-minded people don't bring to the table.

When selecting advisory board members for our firm, we focus on attracting and retaining people with backgrounds very different from ours. Most of the members come from different industries. We also try to find mentors and advisers with views that are different from ours on issues as core as politics and religion. If we know they care about us and have our best interests at heart, they may expand our thinking. When we are genuinely interested in learning about their opinions and what is behind them, we usually discover new information.

We have discussed in this book the importance of replacing judgment with curiosity, and we know that this approach enables you to build relationships that will offer opportunities to step up and lead. When you feel yourself shutting down to someone else, it's a signal for you to say, "Tell me more about that. What do you mean by that? Where does that idea come from? What has your experience been?" Such an approach will likely help you forge a connection that makes it easier to *catalyze change*. People have a hard time shifting their views or positions if you create polarization; this is precisely the moment when someone needs to step up and generate a spirit of interest and collaboration. We want that "someone" to be you.

An extreme example of replacing judgment with curiosity involves the practice of torture. When an interrogator tortures a prisoner, the prisoner talks and talks quickly—but will say anything to stop the torture. But when an interrogator sits down and communicates *respect* for the prisoner's intelligence by saying something like, "Your life has changed for the worse and permanently. You did a bad thing. We caught you. We won. You lost. You are never getting out again. That is a fact. I *do* have some influence over what kind of facility you're going to wind up spending the rest of your life in, what kind of visitation, what quality of food you will receive, and maybe even the kind of linens you will get. What I need from you is some of the information that you have. And I can help you if you help me first."

Torture does not elicit the same quality of information as an interrogation does, because the latter approach is emotionally intelligent and collaborative. It's one that uses curiosity instead of judgment.

The mistakes in your organization are probably less intense than those of a criminal or terrorist. But the principle that curiosity builds relationships and yields better-quality information holds true for those less-intense situations as well. If replacing judgment with curiosity works for interrogating a prisoner, it will work for you too. In one case, for example, a client organization stopped judging and blaming their suppliers for a supply chain problem and faced the fact that their procurement system was broken.

Learn New Things

Because the environment in which your organization operates is in a constant state of change, the organization must change with the environment. As we said earlier, "organizational change" is a misnomer in that organizations don't change unless the people do. To keep up with the times and with ever-changing demands, you will need to learn new skills. We see skill and competency building as an art, and in a way, the ability to learn and adapt is a competency unto itself.

Make it a habit to ask yourself regularly, "What new skill am I learning this month? In what aspect of my life am I pushing myself beyond my comfort zone?" Read subjects that you have not read before; play games you've never played. Go to see things you would not ordinarily see: an opera, an art exhibit, a sporting event. Go talk to your company's interns or entry-level employees about what they are experiencing and what they think your company could do differently. Then go learn about that "new" thing they are looking to you to leverage. If you have focused on business learning up until now, learn to play a musical instrument or learn a new language. This type of activity will do more to improve the flexibility of your mind than continuing to deepen your business knowledge.

Become Comfortable with Uncertainty

During a conversation with Henry, Soren Kaplan, author of the book *Leapfrogging: Harness the Power of Surprise for Business Breakthroughs*, suggested that "In order to create breakthroughs that positively surprise others, we need to first experience surprise ourselves, as part of the process." In other words, we must become comfortable with uncertainty in order to inspire and incite others to change and, perhaps more important, innovate our way through change. Of course, you must practice being in uncomfortable situations in order to eventually become comfortable in them.

Henry experienced this when he first entered a mixed martial arts gym in Albuquerque, New Mexico. Coming from a competitive stand-up background and having won a couple of championships, Henry felt very assured. Upon seeing how comfortable he was fighting in a standing position, his coach Greg Jackson said, "Henry, you appear to be very good on your feet."

Henry replied, "I try to be."

Jackson then said, "Great! We're going to have you spend the next few weeks starting on your hands and knees with a guy on your back. He'll already have one arm over your shoulder getting ready to apply a choke. I want you to get comfortable defending that."

Henry protested, "I'm an expert standing; I wouldn't know what to do on the ground."

Jackson replied, "Henry, I'm asking you to stay on the ground and practice until you are competent and comfortable."

Henry spent the next few (painful) weeks making the transition from being afraid, anxious, and in a bit of physical pain, to being strategic, breathing calmly, and constantly looking for a way to win from that disadvantageous position. In order to change, he had to practice being in an uncomfortable situation—one filled with uncertainty—in order to become comfortable in that same situation.

It is this kind of change—becoming comfortable with people, situations, and environments in which one previously felt uncomfortable—that we try to catalyze in our coaching clients and the leadership teams that we work to develop. Accept your strengths, and work on developing new ones. This begins with a general openness to change and a willingness to be "comfortably uncomfortable."

Discover a Need for Change

The consequences of operating with unchallenged assumptions are often at the root of our clients' interpersonal issues. Many of them have found the following process useful in determining where there is a need for change. We recommend that you try it now. Fill out the worksheet in Figure 4.1 with the vital facts and assumptions that are important to your relationship with a key stakeholder at work (colleague, boss, report, customer, and so on).

When you have filled out the boxes, ask these questions:

1. **What things (opinions, values, beliefs, perspectives, background, fears, hopes, dreams . . .) does this person *know* about me?**
    - How can I tell if the person really knows these things?
    - How do I communicate them to the person?

Figure 4.1 Reality Check Worksheet

1. What things (opinions, values, beliefs, perspectives, background, fears, hopes, dreams ...) does this person *know* about me?
2. What do I *know* about this person?
3. What does this person *assume* about me?
4. What do I *assume* about this person?

- Is it possible (*not* reasonable) for the person to misinterpret these things (or some of them) or to hold an alternative view?
- What are the implications of the person's misinterpretation or misunderstanding of these things about me?

2. **What do I *know* about this person?**
   - What evidence do I really have to support this view?
   - Have I ever openly discussed this with him or her?
   - How could I confirm this fact/opinion?
3. **What does this person *assume* about me?**
   - Is this assumption helpful? If so, how can I confirm it or provide evidence to the person to support it?
   - If this assumption is unhelpful, how can I change it?
   - How can I find out whether he or she is assuming something else entirely?
4. **What do I *assume* about this person?**
   - What if I am wrong?
   - What evidence do I have to support my assumption?
   - How can I find out?

Working through these questions will give you a good indication of where you need to challenge or validate your assumptions and is a great starting point to changing how you interact with others. People who use this process usually find one or two ways that their own behavior has caused a miscommunication or misunderstanding. Once they change the way they themselves have been contributing to the misunderstanding, the relationship changes for the better.

Summary of Key Learnings in Chapter Four

- Organizations don't change until their people change. The ability to change is a core competency required in today's operating environment.
- Moments of leadership present themselves when the people around you are stuck in old ways of thinking and behaving.

- Catalyzing change in others requires that you become comfortable with changing yourself.
- Before you can be effective at stepping up in leadership moments, you must become adept at **questioning your own mental models** and **avoiding selective perception (cognitive bias)**. These are the two mechanisms that protect you against uncomfortable feelings. In other words, you must become comfortable with ambiguity.
- Operating with unchallenged assumptions is often at the root of interpersonal issues.

Your Next Steps to Step Up and Catalyze Change in Yourself and Others

- Examine whether your company or industry had a reliable and/or sustainable advantage or "source" in the past that you've become used to. Is this likely to change in the future—or has it already? How does this affect your company?
- Think of an instance when you (or your group or company) were reluctant to change (the way Microsoft was in being "late to the game" with changes in computers). How did it affect you—and how would you do this differently going forward? Identify some concrete steps you can take to prevent this from happening again.
- Choose a future project or initiative for which you can challenge assumptions and encourage your team to do the same. Ask your team, "What are the paradigms within which we operate?" Conduct a "paradigm-busting" session that challenges the sacred cows in your organization.
- Have your team undergo the 5 Whys process with a particular event, scenario, project, or the like.
- Conduct a 360-degree feedback process for yourself and your team. Use the approach discussed in the "Get Assessed" sec-

tion of this chapter (examining feedback and asking colleagues for their support by having them notify you if you "slip up" and congratulate you when you do better). You can do this informally, or have a reliable firm come in and do it for you with a formal assessment process.

- Hold a meeting or gathering where you ask the magic wand question of your team or organization. Answer it about yourself; have team members do the same.

Step Up Link

Reality Check Worksheet

CHAPTER FIVE

Leverage Pessimism

Beware of false knowledge; it is more dangerous than ignorance.
—George Bernard Shaw

Our Promise

The power of positive thinking has received a great deal of attention in the mana gement literature and the popular press. In fact, the belief in positivity has led many people to be suspicious of any form of negativity. People who point out risks or issues are described as Chicken Little, claiming that the sky is falling down.

But what if the sky really *is* falling down? What if your group or organization is facing real challenges of which you are not aware? Worse still, what if some people in your group or organization are aware of these issues—but you are not listening to them? In this chapter, we will discuss the value of the pessimist's perspective and how to leverage the wisdom contained in negativity. Leveraging pessimism is like taking medicine; you don't have to like it, but you have to do it.

Recognize the Moment

We have all worked with "George." He is a nice guy and pretty good at his job. However, whenever someone suggests something new or there's a setback, George goes into overdrive. He is a real glass-half-empty guy, a dyed-in-the-wool pessimist who can see only the problems and obstacles associated with any change initiative. He drives the rest of the team crazy, and his pessimism can kill the mood in a meeting. Others see him as conservative, risk-averse, and resistant to change. Dealing with all that negativity is so draining that some of his colleagues avoid George or find ways to work around him; they fear being sucked into a death spiral of negativity. George, however, does not see things that way. In fact, George is frustrated at the continuing failure to adequately risk-assess and risk-assure decisions. He worries that those around him get carried away with one crazy idea after another. Sometimes George feels that he is the only voice of reason left in the building!

George and his teammates' exchanges show us what happens when optimists and pessimists interact in an emotionally unintelligent way. The misunderstanding of each other's inherent biases leads each side to undervalue the other side's perspective and potential value. This leads to frustration and ultimately the dreaded *Vortex*, in which frustration creates more negativity, and so on. The Vortex operates like a black hole for an organization's energy, creativity, and, ultimately, performance. Take a moment to think about your own organization. Do you work with a George? Are there mood vampires in your organization who are capable of sucking the life out of any interaction? If you have been trying (and failing) to make these people more positive, we suggest that you may be missing the point somewhat. Pessimists have their place and can create real value in your organization, but not by your making them me-too optimists.

Calculate the Burn Rate

These situations aren't just unpleasant for groups and organization; they actually pose a resource problem. We explain this to

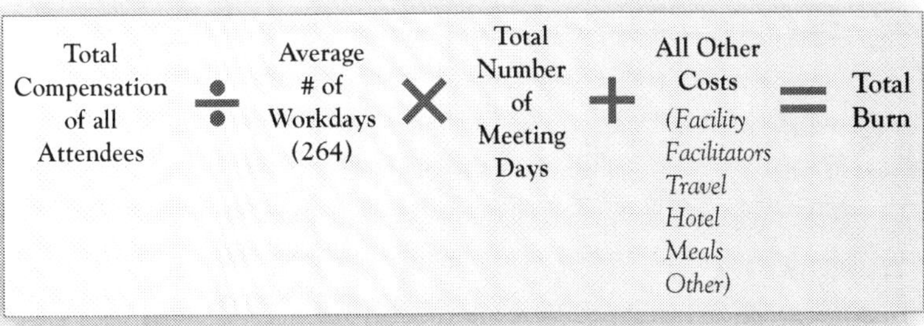

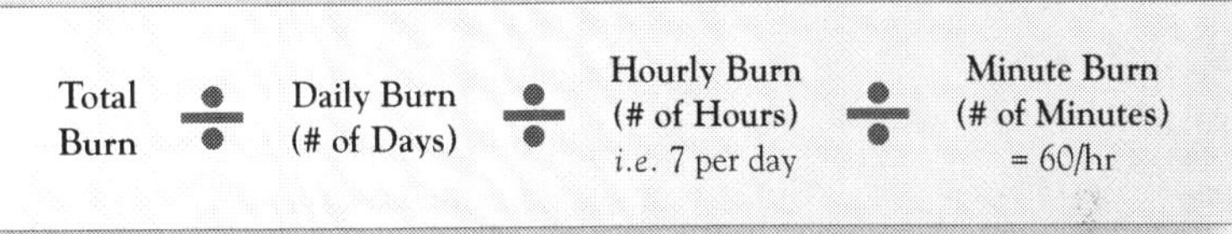

Figure 5.1 Calculate the Burn Rate
Copyright © Dynamic Results, LLC

our clients by citing a *burn rate* (see Figure 5.1)—that is, a way to quantify the financial expense of our meeting time with them. Here is an example:

- Divide the total compensation of all the client's employees attending the meeting by 264 (the average number of U.S. workdays per year).
- Multiply the result by the number of days that the meeting will last.
- Add the cost of the facility in which the meeting is being held, our fees for facilitation of the meeting, hotel and travel costs, and so on.
- Divide the result by the number of days, hours, or minutes that the meeting will consume.

For example, imagine nine executives with compensation totaling $2,340,000 per year. Dividing that figure by 264 equals $8,863 per day for their time. Add $7,500 in airfare and lodging for a two-day meeting, plus $2,000 for the meeting room and meals. You now have a rate of $13,613 per day (plus our facilitation fees). This is $1,701.63 per meeting hour and $28.36 per meeting minute.

Calculating the burn rate makes it easy to quantify the financial expense of getting sucked into the Vortex and passing that point of no return—in this case, $28.36 per wasted minute. What about the other expenses, though? Everyone is burning emotional and mental energy getting sucked into this particular Vortex, and all of the resources used will be gone forever.

We've all had conversations that prompted us to think, "I'll never get *those* twenty minutes of my life back." Wherever you are on the organization chart, your job is to recognize when your money is being invested wisely in solution-oriented discussions and to help the group that you are with to steer clear of event horizons.

The Three P's

Optimism expert Martin Seligman has explained the difference between optimists and pessimists in terms of how they explain events, both good and bad, to themselves and to others as well. Seligman notes that when bad things happen, pessimists tend to think in terms of what he calls the Three P's to explain negative events:

- **Permanent.** A pessimist tends to see a problem as something that won't change, whereas an optimist can view it as a temporary setback.
- **Pervasive.** A pessimist thinks globally; the issue has implications beyond this specific incident. In contrast, an optimist

tends to see the problem as related only to the specific isolated event.
- **Personal.** A pessimist assumes personal blame, whereas an optimist sees a broader picture.

Let's take an example of a how a pessimist might view a work project that did not go well:

- I will never be able to do this . . . never have . . . never will. (permanent)
- The project failed because I'm just not good with people. (pervasive)
- I totally screwed this up. (personal)

An optimist might think:

- OK, it didn't work out this time, but I hope it can work out next time if we change a few things.
- This part of my project didn't work out, but other parts are fine.
- I accept my part in this failure, but it wasn't all down to me; there were real mitigating factors at play.

Optimists and pessimists also tend to switch these perspectives when they look at a positive outcome. An optimist enjoying a positive event is likely to explain it in terms that are permanent, pervasive, and personal. He is likely to say something like, "I succeeded on this project due to an ability I have that I could apply to a new and different situation." The pessimist, in contrast, tends to dismiss the result: "I didn't do that much. It was just the luck of the day, and if the situation changed even a little, I probably couldn't repeat the performance."

Pessimism Is Not a Disease

The value and utility of an optimistic perspective has been written about extensively. For example, optimism has been found to link to high performance, especially in sales contexts, likely because of the optimist's response to the continuous rejection that salespeople face.[1] As we say in the martial arts world, "You don't lose when you get knocked down; you lose when you choose not to get back up!"

It is certainly true that optimists are easier to be around and create a more pleasant and nurturing environment. And as Henry often says, "Pessimists are often right and rarely happy," a phenomenon referred to by psychologists as *depressive realism*. Pessimists constantly say things like, "I told you we couldn't do that" and "I told you we'd get fired by that client" and "I knew we'd be late."

Pessimists get a bad rap. Yes, they can be a true pain in the ass, but they also point out problems and shed light on tough issues that others may be avoiding. You may be undervaluing pessimists; they can actually serve a purpose and have a role to play in your organization. However, we *don't* think that pessimists should be in leadership roles. No one wants to be on a team led by someone who is telling them they will lose the game, before the game has even begun. In fact, our extensive experience in assessing and developing leaders has led us to conclude that the best leaders are optimists who have good reality testing. They say things like, "I am fully aware of the challenges we will face, but in spite of that, I am confident that this team can deliver."

Pessimism is not a disease, nor does it represent pathological behavior. Rather, the issues associated with the Vortex occur because of miscommunication and misunderstanding between optimists and pessimists; they are not due to the mere existence of differing perspectives.

(We do want to offer some advice to readers who may have a pessimistic bias. You will often point out troubling issues; and in many cases, the dire consequences you predict will in fact come to pass. When this happens, we urge you to resist using the four words that are arguably the most toxic in the English language: "I told you so." It is almost impossible to say or think this without a tone of triumphalism, which will destroy your relationship with the person to whom you say it. No matter how justified you feel in saying "I told you so," please think long and hard to come up with better wording, such as, "I tried to alert us to this danger, but I clearly didn't explain myself very well. How can I change the way I present these risks so that we can take them on board in the future?")

Optimism Is Not the Same as Positivity

So, to avoid the Vortex—and to understand and value your company's "George"—we need to discuss the nature of mood and of positive and negative bias.

People tend to use the terms *emotion* and *mood* interchangeably, but they're truly very different. Human beings experience a vast range of emotions, such as anger, elation, pride, and disgust. These tend to have a specific cause, last for a short period, and have a distinct physiological signature, generally a facial expression. Emotions also tend to create an urge to act. There's usually a reason when you are angry; others can see it in your face, and you want to confront the source of your anger.

Mood is a much more subtle phenomenon. Moods tend to range on a continuum from positive to negative, but seem to be confined to this one dimension. So although there are many emotions we can feel (happy, sad, surprised, fearful, disgusted, and so on), for mood there is only the positive–negative dimension, and that is pretty much it. There tends not to be a specific cause for a mood; your mood may not be apparent to others from your facial expressions, and it can last a long time. Pessimists seem to be especially prone to negative mood and may even have a generally negative bias.

Optimism is not the same as positivity, and pessimism is not the same as negativity. It is possible to be an optimist and have a slightly negative bias; you can see the trouble ahead but are confident in your ability to overcome obstacles and achieve a good result. This is preferable to being an optimist with a very positive bias, as those are the type of people who walk into glass doors. The idea that there might be a door in their way doesn't strike them, at least not until the door does! So although it was an optimist who invented the airplane, it was a pessimist who invented the parachute.

Optimists and people with a positive bias see a munificent and benign universe where good things generally happen. People with a negative bias tend to focus primarily on the bad experiences in life—and this perception of the world colors their reality. These people are not *inventing* issues and obstacles; rather, they tend to be sensitized to these issues and more likely to see problems than do people with a positive bias. People with a negative bias look for things that stand out as wrong, whereas people with a positive bias tend to look for things that match. Remember those old "spot the difference" pictures in magazines? People with a negative bias tend to be quite good at those!

To illustrate how people with differing biases can get sucked into the Vortex by misinterpreting each other's perspective, let's look at a few scenarios. The first is a discussion about a person. John, who has a positive bias, is discussing Patricia's performance with his colleague George (who we know has a negative bias).

George: We are still not getting the quality of analysis from Patricia that we need. Did you speak with her about that?

John: Yes, several times, and I can see she is really trying on this one. It's a new role for her, and it will take time for her to get comfortable with all the new challenges.

George: But John, it's been six months now. You need to seriously consider whether she's right for this role.

John: I understand your frustration, but I am sure she will be great if we give her more time. To be fair, I probably haven't spent enough quality time with her on this initiative.

The seeds of the Vortex are being sown underneath this very polite conversation. John probably thinks that George gives up too easily on people and doesn't understand the need to nurture, grow, and develop employees. He finds George's negative attitude to be a real downer. In fact, John's positive bias compels him to give people a second, third, and even fourth chance to succeed.

George has a very different perspective—and explanation. He thinks that John is ducking the hard calls and is on another of his crusades or rescue missions. George believes that the company and even Patricia herself would be happier if everyone accepted the simple fact that she is not up to the job, and found someone who is. George doesn't think John is doing Patricia any favors by insisting that she persevere in a role for which she is unsuitable.

When positive and negative perspectives clash like this, the participants can lose respect for each other—which can start them down a slippery slope.

Our second example is one in which John and George are discussing a business proposal. John presents what he believes to be a good plan, and George immediately dives in to point out all the flaws and issues that the plan faces. John is upset and angry and thinks, *Nothing is ever good enough for that guy. All he does is point out flaws and weaknesses. He must have a black belt in criticism.*

However, people like George see more value in looking for and pointing out negatives. They are highly sensitized to drawbacks and feel that they would not be doing their job if they didn't try to help by spotting the idea's gaps and getting them filled. George believes that ideas, like people, are forged in adversity or crucibles; ideas are built through critique, and focusing on the positives is just cheerleading. He notices how crushed and sullen John becomes and wonders about his intestinal fortitude. John and George are likely to repeat this pattern: George offers critiques while John experiences criticism, and neither is happy with the other's behavior.

Let's turn the situation around and have George present an idea to John. John points out all the good stuff and says how great the plan is, based on his positively biased belief that you should support and nurture people in order to bring out the best in them. At the end of the conversation, John says something like, "Overall, I love this plan. However, it could be even better if you included some market research." George leaves the meeting a little frustrated, thinking that he never gets any real constructive criticism from John—giving him nothing to work with. He was expecting some negative comments, because he can see several flaws with the plan. He assumed that John must not have really read it, as he didn't point them out.

They discuss the plan again during their next meeting. John is surprised that George still hasn't included any market research and has to ask for it again. George is taken aback. The mention of market research, which John added at the very end of their discussion, seemed like a throwaway comment to George. He didn't see it as a gap in the original plan, but rather as an optional extra. Surely if it had been important, John would have made more of an issue of it the first time. Once again we can see how this pattern, if repeated, can lead to a breakdown of trust and respect between the parties.

One last example involves what is often called the "feedback sandwich": you give someone a positive comment, then say a negative comment, and then finish with another positive comment. Though frequently cited as a good way to give a critique, this process fails to recognize the perspectives of positively and negatively biased people. Giving a feedback sandwich to someone with a positive bias doesn't work because she only hears the first and last part; she focuses on and remembers the positives. Someone with a negative bias has an even worse time; she focuses only on the negative and feels that you are trying to manipulate her by bookending the comment with false positives.

If you have a negative comment to make, just make it clearly and succinctly—and do the same with a positive comment. Keep the two conversations separate; don't blend them. That way, if you *do* compliment someone, he will understand that it is not a prelude to a negative comment—even if he has a negative bias.

Empathy Is Critical

We have discussed the nature of pessimism in some depth because in order to leverage pessimism, you need to be able to empathize with those who hold pessimistic views. Empathy is about *feelings*, not facts. Being empathic requires you to express understanding of how another person feels and to do so in a way that he or she recognizes. This is not always easy to do, but the following story illustrates just how important it can be to do it.

Henry consulted to top-secret facilities in the national defense arena for the United States and its allies. When doing strategic planning or conflict resolution work, he was presented with what were described as "technical disagreements" with key stakeholders, such as customers or development partners. Sometimes the scenarios did indeed sound like technical issues. In most cases, however, what were couched as technical challenges were actually *relationship* challenges; they were primarily *feeling* based, not fact based.

This client was responsible for developing a technology that would help detect and deter terrorism for a military branch of the U.S. government. The team of engineers and physicists involved were not just best in class; they were *the class.* They invented the technology and had the only capability in the world to develop, maintain, and improve that particular system. Their staff comprised the second-highest concentration of IQ in a single population on the planet.

Their customer, an oversight agency in the U.S. government, was extremely combative in the relationship and frequently criticized the work. The agency continually questioned our client's technical ability and commitment and threatened to reduce funding.

Our client complained that although the customer was expert at knowing what to look for, where to look for it, and how to respond when terror targets were found, they did not have any technical expertise. They therefore had no legitimate basis to question our client's ability to deliver a reliable product.

Our client wanted us to incorporate a strategy for convincing the customer that they were technical experts. They would measure our success in part by the amount of additional funding they received from their customer.

The word "trust" kept coming up during our needs assessment. It wasn't always stated overtly, but it was clearly an issue. And the issue wasn't that our client lacked the technical ability to deliver; it was that their customer was highly pessimistic about their competence and didn't trust them.

They needed a different approach. We asked our client to stop focusing exclusively on the technical arguments and instead to assemble a team of people who were good at building relationships with customers. We suggested that if they got interested in what their military customer was *feeling* more than what they were *thinking*, we might be able to find a way to become a trusted adviser, rather than just a "vendor" or "supplier."

This was a challenge for our client, a group of almost exclusively male technically minded and analytical people. Their military customer had a command-and-control mentality: "You work for me, so do what I say." Neither our client nor their customer were accustomed to or interested in exploring feelings.

Our client allowed us to find the people in their organization who were good at building relationships, regardless of their technical ability, and then have those people focus on relationship building with their customer.

Our client had been ignoring Einstein's definition of insanity: doing the same thing over and over and expecting a different result. For almost twenty years, they had their best technical people argue to their customer that their designs were best in class. It just so happened that the people who were the best technically were, in almost all cases, introverts who didn't have well-developed relationship-building skills.

The pessimists among our client's people, some of them world-renowned technical wizards and fathers of their technologies, said things like, "Our client is stupid; they don't know anything about what we do or how we do it, and I refuse to try to reason with idiots." They also had a leader and a few key players on the leadership team who immediately saw the logic in our suggestion and agreed to try it. For the first time in the organization's history, they launched an initiative dedicated exclusively to *building a relationship* with a customer. They created focus groups, conducted one-on-one interviews, found advocates in areas of influence, spent nontransactional time with the client, and, perhaps most important, dedicated specific people to *understanding how their customer was feeling* toward them.

Once our client took that all-important step of replacing judgment with curiosity, they realized that their customer was in a very tough spot. The president of the United States, the U.S. Congress, various branches of our military and intelligence communities, and our allied nations were all concerned about and felt dedicated to resolving a particular kind of threat. The intensity of this desire increased dramatically after the 9/11 attacks, and one individual in our client's customer organization was the actual human responsible for seeing that this technology was designed and deployed in a way that worked. He worried that the world would be more vulnerable to terrorist threats if our client missed certain deadlines. Because he didn't have the technical expertise to design or fully understand the system's inner workings himself, he sometimes felt ill-equipped to explain it to others. To make matters worse, the technical people he had to deal with in our client organization emanated a passive undercurrent of disrespect toward him. It made him feel as though they thought he was stupid and unqualified to discuss the system from a technical perspective. Of course, it wasn't surprising that he felt that way, as that was *exactly* what they thought.

Our client responded brilliantly. Now that they understood how their customer felt, they could be more empathic when addressing the concerns—as well as some of their own dysfunction. They started using a different set of criteria to select people to interface with their customer. Rather than choosing subject-matter experts, they chose great relationship builders: good speakers and presenters who were empathic and solution oriented and who possessed enough technical expertise to answer basic questions.

Their new approach generated outstanding results. In a span of eighteen months, the customer abandoned their combative approach. They no longer kept our client out of key meetings or threatened decreased funding. Instead, they openly advocated for our client in Washington, treated them as trusted advisers, came to them for advice before making budgeting decisions, included them in important meetings, and *increased* funding to them before it was solicited. Our client's technical ability hadn't changed at all, but their interest in how other people—highly pessimistic people—were feeling *did* change.

As we've noted elsewhere in this book, people respond to and interact with us based on what they think of us, not on what *we think they should think* of us. We must care about how they feel, express our understanding of that, and—once we've acknowledged the other person's feelings—move on to the facts.

Examine the key projects you are running right now. Ask yourself if the people managing those projects for you have the right balance of technical and people skills. You can also apply this approach to your products or services. Here's how. Take your top three products and conduct a features-and-benefits exercise. Features are the technical characteristics of the product. Your salespeople tend to focus on them (this is why our customers should want our product). Benefits are the problems that your product solves for your customer. If you have problems distinguishing the features from the benefits, or if you feel that the customer voice is difficult to discern, you may want to consider whether you are overly focusing on the technical aspects of your offering and ignoring the relationship dimension with your customers. An inability to perceive and value the other person's perspective is toxic in business, whether that "other person" is a customer, colleague, supplier, or other stakeholder, as our client found out almost too late. Empathy is a powerful antidote to the kind of misunderstanding that destroys relationships.

Step Up

Embracing another's perspective requires a genuinely empathic understanding. Empathy is an extremely important but misunderstood skill; it's been called the "secret sauce" of leadership.[2] Many people equate empathy with the idea of "walking a mile in another person's shoes." They ask themselves what they would feel like in a particular situation and try to relate to the other person on the basis of that understanding. This is an oddly egocentric approach and not really what empathy is about. We've had the pleasure of working alongside some of the pioneers in the science of emotional intelligence while speaking alongside them at conferences for emotional intelligence assessors. These colleagues, psychologists Peter Salovey (president of Yale University) and David Caruso (whose work we cited in Chapter One), explain true empathy like this:[3]

- Recognizing the other person's emotion
- Re-creating that emotion in yourself to understand what is going on for the other person
- Relating to the person in the light of that understanding

Simply put, empathy is not about asking yourself what *you* would feel like in a given situation; it requires that you ask, "In what situations do I feel like *that?*" (angry, frustrated, disappointed, and so on). Knowing how the emotion in question affects your perspective and worldview allows you to constructively relate to someone in that emotional state.

So when you read the suggestions in the next sections for dealing with and leveraging pessimism, try to ensure that you are deploying them empathically. Remember that the pessimist or negatively biased person is working hard to point out what she considers to be real dangers and potential problems, so her perspective is worth considering. If *you* are the negatively biased person, you must also work to understand your positively biased colleagues' view and ensure that you communicate in a way they'll hear. When discussing a business proposal with a colleague, you could say something like, "Here is what I like about your plan. I can see how it addresses some of our major problems. However, there are a few areas where I still have some concerns. I may have missed how these are being covered; let's discuss those issues now so that we can understand if there are any real gaps we need to address."

Pessimists Have Their Place

There are specific ways to keep pessimists in their place and appreciate their contribution (sometimes by publicly thanking and/or acknowledging them for getting your group to address critical issues and considerations). You should also leverage the "state it once" method so that they don't paralyze the organization. (Although you might guess how this method works, we will explain it in Chapter Six.) To emphasize a point we frequently make: pessimists should have a role in the organization, be shown appreciation, and not be in leadership roles.

Some Conflict Is Healthy

When a group of people has prematurely agreed on an idea, it is the pessimist who brings the gift of conflict to the party. But you don't have to be a pessimist to generate constructive conflict. This is a leadership moment; anyone can step up. Remember what you learned in Chapter Two: that performance rises as conflict rises, but only up to a point. At that point, performance drops as conflict becomes dysfunctional (see Figure 2.1).

Take the example of a team that needs to come up with a creative strategy to address a business issue. Most organizations dial up the positivity by getting a high-energy brainstorm going; however, this is only part of the solution. Opportunities to step up exist throughout the process of addressing an issue. You'll recall from Chapter One that there are four types of emotional states that are suited to various tasks (see the Mood and Cognition Model, Figure 1.2). You could use them in the following sequence in order to produce a workable creative proposal:

Step 1 (high energy, positive): conduct your high-energy, positive brainstorm to generate lots of ideas.

Step 2 (low energy, positive): drop the energy level to consider all of the ideas you have generated and to gain consensus on the more promising ones.

Step 3 (low energy, negative): leverage your pessimists to point out the challenges, risks, and flaws in your options so as to put together the most robust, risk-aware plan.

Step 4 (high energy, negative): generate a little anger to get the team moving to action mode.

You need to use both positive and negative emotion to develop an implementable plan. If you don't appreciate and utilize your pessimists, you'll end up pursuing plans that have no realistic chance of success.

Ask, "Is It True?"

One of the emotional intelligence competencies we assess and develop in people is called *reality testing*, a person's ability to objectively see a situation for what it is without coloring it with his or her own emotional filters. Emotional intelligence is dynamic; it ebbs and flows in all of us. We all have good days and bad days—even good and bad hours, minutes, and meetings. People don't always know when they're having a day of high or low reality testing, so we have a developmental strategy for clients to use when they are experiencing a strong emotional response to a situation. Our goal is to have them apply this strategy before they make a major decision and while still experiencing the strong emotions. We call the practice "Is it true?"

Suppose you begin to perceive that a colleague is incapable of doing something competently or is "out to get you." Before you react to your strong feelings of disgust or fear, ask yourself, "Is it true?" or perhaps, "What *other explanation* is possible here?" Remember, people are emotional first and rational second. Asking, "Is it true?" helps you return to a more objective state. Colm challenged one of his coaching clients to question his assumptions about a peer's seemingly constant criticism of his ideas by asking such questions as, "Does he challenge you in public or in private?" The client realized that he perceived his peer as a foe when, in fact, his peer was simply challenging him to improve and grow.

Insert Some Pessimism

When discussions in meetings get sucked into the Vortex, the potential of the collective is being financially, energetically, and creatively drained away. Your investment in one-on-one meetings and interactions works the same way. You know how crucial it is to address real issues, confront people and situations when required, and leverage pessimism for the benefit of the organization. At some point, however—and by failing to work on a solution—you may be (albeit passively) choosing to allow the organization to pay for an investment in negative, redundant dialogue. Think of the difference between constructive and destructive pessimism as the difference between playing devil's advocate and being the devil himself.

Again, pessimism properly leveraged can increase individual and team performance. So sometimes, when you're interacting with happy people—everyone getting along and fully aligned, nobody exploring other possibilities—you may want to be the person who steps up and inserts some pessimism to stimulate thinking. Doing so might require that you ask the people around you such questions as

- What if we're wrong about this?
- What else might be possible?
- What might others say about this?

Conduct a "Pre-Mortem"

We sometimes advise our clients to imagine that it is three years from now, the project they're working on has failed horribly, and they now have to explain why that happened. What issues or challenges got in the way? We also encourage people to identify all the barriers or hurdles that they'll have to overcome to succeed in their plan. Some of our resolutely positive clients worry that this exercise will kill the enthusiasm in the room. However, identifying *real* challenges is different from inventing imagined ones. And problems never simply disappear just because you have refused to acknowledge them.

When Feelings Are Facts

It is particularly difficult to relate to another person's feelings when you think that he has his facts wrong—especially when he seems impenetrable in his opinions or beliefs. But feelings *are facts* to the people feeling them. They may be having a strong negative intuition—a bad feeling about a project, client, or prospective new hire. Although it's tempting to dismiss these misgivings as "just" feelings, they're very real to the person experiencing them—and you potentially cause two problems if you do dismiss them. First, you damage your relationship with the person by not respecting his intuition. Second, you lose the chance to explore the risks or challenges he is sensing but that he may not necessarily be able to articulate.

Try to remember a time when this person pointed out a challenge that you may have missed or not sufficiently prepared for. Now you can relate to him by saying something like, "Your hunches about this stuff have proven to be useful in the past. I think we should fully discuss your concerns so that I can understand what I may be missing. I don't expect you to be able to specifically identify the issue, so let's do that together now." If a team member consistently brings up concerns you believe to be unfounded, there are two possible explanations. One is that the person is a complete "negative Nellie" whose opinion you should ignore. The second is that your own opinions or worldview are impervious to his perspective. You should give equal consideration to both of these possibilities.

How to Handle Objections

The objections that people raise to ideas, plans, or processes are often openings to the Vortex; that is, they can lead a conversation down a negative path. We have developed a five-step process for responding to such objections, which will help you avoid being sucked into the Vortex. We have successfully used this process with our clients and invite you to try it for yourself. Figure 5.2 illustrates the steps graphically, and we describe each in the next sections.

Step 1: Listen/Inquire

Henry once heard a mentor say, "Listening takes place when the other person is talking." Remember what we said in Chapter

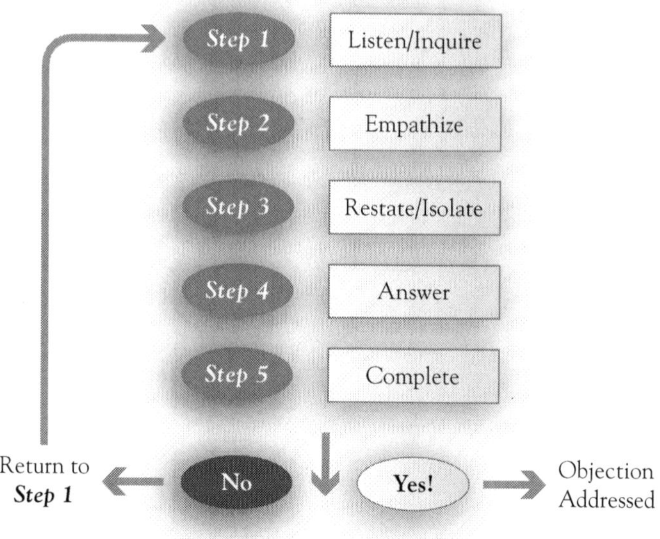

Figure 5.2 Objection-Handling Process
Copyright © Dynamic Results, LLC

Two: listening is not the same as being quiet or quietly rehearsing what you want to say while another person is speaking. Make sure you understand the objection thoroughly before moving on to the remaining steps. Ask a question that gets the person to fully express her point of view.

Step 2: Empathize

Speak to feelings before you speak to facts. Express your understanding of how the other person feels even if her facts are wrong. A simple, "I can see that you are frustrated," or something similar, will do. Remember that empathy is about the expression of your understanding of how the other person feels.

This requires you to be vulnerable and allow yourself to feel what she is feeling.

Step 3: Isolate and Restate

The person making the objection may have mentioned five things going wrong with her day, but she probably came to you to discuss only one. She might have said, "My dog threw up on my shoes while I was leaving the house, my car wouldn't start, I was stuck in traffic, and you are late getting me that report I needed." That last item is clearly the one that concerns you. So your blended empathy and restatement might sound like, "Wow, I've had days like that too, and know what that pressure feels like. I wish I could help you with the dog, the car, and your commute. It sounds like I let you down by not getting you this report; I could improve your situation by getting it to you."

Step 4: Answer

This is the step most people skip to as soon as they hear a problem: offering an immediate opinion or solution. We want you to have navigated the first three steps before taking this one—where you tell the person what you will or won't do for her. This step may require you to tell people the precise answer they didn't want to hear, such as, "I know you may not have wanted to hear this, and here is what we've decided to do." For example, you might give a response like, "I know I promised to have that information available for the sales call yesterday. I dropped the ball and the sales call is over, so I won't be able to make good on that commitment." Or "I really thought that was the right thing for us to do at the time I made the commitment. Upon reflection, I changed my mind and should have come to speak with you about the change in perspective when it occurred. I'm no longer committed to doing it, and I'm sorry I didn't tell you sooner."

Step 5: Complete

Check in to see if you have resolved the situation to the best of your ability. You might not have been able to give the person what she wanted; has she accepted that? Is she willing to move on? If yes, you are done. If not, go right back to step one and ask her to tell you what else you can do to take care of her.

Recognize When Enough Is Enough

The leader is the person who identifies when the group is coming closer to a discussion's black hole and redirects them before their financial and energetic resources get sucked into the Vortex. In a sense, you are like the captain of a spaceship. You need to bring your ship close enough to the black hole so that you can observe and measure it for the purpose of navigating around it. However, you have to accomplish this without going too far, or you will get sucked in—bringing the ship and everyone on it with you.

You can redirect a discussion using our "state it once" concept. Say something like, "Now that we've identified the problem, what should we do about it?" We will have more to say about "state it once" in the next chapter.

Summary of Key Learnings in Chapter Five

- Both optimists and pessimists tend to misunderstand each other's inherent biases. This leads each side to undervalue the other's perspective and potential value added.
- People with a negative bias don't *invent* issues and obstacles to put in the way. Rather, they tend to be sensitized to these issues, so they are more likely to see problems than are people with a positive bias.
- In order to leverage pessimism, you must be able to empathize with those who hold pessimistic views.

- Empathy involves recognizing another's emotion, recreating that emotion in yourself to understand what is going on for the other person, and relating to the person in the light of that understanding—and in a way that he or she recognizes.
- Empathize with people *before* you dive into debate or the dissection of facts.
- You want some degree of pessimism in your meetings and should appreciate the people who consistently bring pessimism to the table.
- Those same pessimists, though always appreciated, should not be in leadership roles.

Your Next Steps to Step Up and Leverage Pessimism in Your Organization

- Select your top three strategic priorities and conduct a premortem on each.
- Identify a George in your organization or group. Make an effort to understand, appreciate, and utilize his point of view going forward, knowing that he's keeping an eye out for holes in the plans. Create opportunities to appropriately introduce this perspective in your meetings.
- Before your next team meeting, identify the person in your group with a negative bias and coach her on how to present her concerns in a way that allows others to hear and *value* her perspective.
- Calculate the burn rate for a given meeting, gathering, trip, or project and present it to your team.
- Apply the five steps of the objection-handling process in an upcoming one-on-one interaction. Make a point of debriefing the process to identify how you can improve your ability to deploy it.

Step Up Link

Objection-Handling Process Graphic

CHAPTER SIX

Reverse Momentum

Don't find fault, find a remedy.
—Henry Ford

Our Promise

In the previous chapter, we showed you how to leverage pessimism and avoid getting stuck in negativity. But pessimism isn't the only thing that gets you stuck. Anyone can get stuck in redundant discussions that seem to be plummeting into a spiral of negativity. Although these discussions are horrible time wasters, they provide you with an opportunity to step up and exercise leadership by being the one with the tools and skills to reverse the negative momentum. This chapter will show you how.

Recognize the Moment

We worked with the CFO of a large bank that was struggling with a major financing deal with a Fortune 100 multinational corporation. Everyone on the CFO's team was highly stressed. They had done deals like this before, but this time the law firm that was handling part of the contract preparation was giving them a bit of trouble. That firm was new to the bank, but the bank's client had insisted that they use them for this deal. Though a very professional and reputable firm, the partner handling the deal—the expert in this type of contract—rubbed people the wrong way. Even the head of the bank's own legal department had begun refusing to deal with him.

To help coach the CFO, we attended one of his team's meetings to observe him in action. We witnessed the team working reasonably well while discussing issues—including the legal bottlenecks—that were delaying the deal. All was going well until near the meeting's end, when one team member mentioned the latest condescending email from the law firm's partner. A forty-minute discussion of the partner's shortcomings as a manager and as a lawyer ensued.

"He is micromanaging his people," said one team member.

"I bet he has OCD," said another.

"How could someone like him ever make partner in a decent firm like that?" wondered a third person.

This was a useful venting exercise, and, given the stress they were all feeling, it actually served a purpose at that point in the team's development. It allowed them to express their emotion together and feel as though they were joined in a common problem.

We talked with the CFO about whether or not this conversation was a good use of the team's time. We agreed that it was probably necessary; teams dealing with a frustrating problem sometimes need to blow off a bit of stream. However, we also acknowledged that it would not serve a good purpose to *repeat* that session. Forty minutes is a long time to spend venting.

We also predicted that the team was likely to vent like this again, because the source of the problem remained—and because it's always easier to apportion blame than to move to constructive solutions that may involve you owning *your* part of the problem. This presented the CFO with an opportunity to step up.

Sure enough, at the next meeting, one of the team launched into a tirade about the partner's behavior, and everyone else settled in for a good download. At this point, the CFO intervened and said, "Guys, I'm as annoyed with him as you all are, and I would also enjoy a chance to beat up on him. But as much fun as it would be, I don't think psychoanalyzing the guy for forty minutes is a good use of our time. Let's let the head of our legal department have a frank conversation with him about his behavior. If that doesn't correct the issue, we'll plan to escalate it to his managing partner. Meanwhile, let's get back to talking about the contract."

The CFO thus stopped the momentum of a redundant and negative conversation, recognizing and stepping up in a leadership moment.

Then he said, "By the way, if anyone wants to have another pop at him, I'm buying drinks tonight. You're all welcome to join me for beer and character assassination!" The team recognized that it was ducking the real issue to dump on the partner, and they got back to discussing the contract. During this session, they began to recognize some of the important issues that the tricky partner was actually raising—problems that his "bad" attitude had caused them to miss.

Look for the following signs of redundant, negative conversations:

- People are repeating a point (particularly something they don't like or are worried about).
- You are having that déjà vu feeling: "We identified this problem last week and didn't do anything about it then."
- You recognize that the subject at hand is outside of your or your team's control or influence.

Calculating the burn rate (described in Chapter Five) for redundant negative conversation will also be useful. It tends to focus people's minds because, whereas the amount of value you might otherwise have created is a highly subjective question, the *actual cost* of having you sitting in a redundant meeting is a hard fact that is pretty inescapable. We keep the burn rate written on the wall or somewhere in plain sight when we are facilitating leadership team development or strategic planning and implementation meetings. We'll sometimes point to it and ask whether the discussion we are currently engaged in is a good use of everyone's time and also a good investment for the organization.

The Unforgiving Culture

Redundant conversations that are carried along and perpetuated by negative momentum often relate to issues about an individual's behavior, as in the case of the law firm partner we referred to earlier. Speaking negatively about someone in your own organization doesn't just waste valuable time; it also damages that individual's reputation. A fundamental component of a person's leadership effectiveness is grounded in what organizational psychologists call *social capital*: the type of reputation and amount of clout and credibility that a person has. This includes the strength of the network that he or she can call on.

As people become more senior in an organization, what they know (their functional expertise) becomes less important, and whom they know—their network of relationships—becomes more important. When you speak negatively about a colleague, or participate with others in speaking negatively about a colleague, you damage that person's reputation and seriously impair his or her potential effectiveness as a leader. Imagine that you have a team member who is consistently late to meetings. If the punctual members of your team were to repeatedly discuss the fact that this one team member is late, you cement her reputation in the organization as a habitually late individual. Eventually, that person might receive feedback from others or recognize on her own that her constant lateness was having a negative impact on the team. She could spend the next year showing up to all meetings on time; but if she were late just once more, other team members would be apt to say something like, "There she goes being late again." Spending this much energy cementing a colleague's negative reputation makes it very hard—impossible in some cultures—for her to undo that reputation, *even if* she changes her performance.

Take a moment to think back over your own career. Have you ever been a victim of negative or disparaging comments? If so, how difficult was it to repair the damage? Think about the last job transition you had. Did the person who took on your old role spend his time telling others what a great job you did and how easy the transition was going to be because of the great foundations you had built? Or did he talk about how challenging it would be? Discussing the difficulties you face in a new role is very common and quite understandable; however, it is not a victimless crime. It comes at the cost of the reputation of the person you're replacing.

If you are a senior player in the organization, people expect you to speak for the organization. So when you label a colleague as "constantly late" or "unreliable" or "difficult," you apply the organization's endorsement to that label. You contribute to an unforgiving enterprise-wide culture that is toxic for leadership growth and development. You alert the organization to a person's developmental gap on the bold assumption that what you are saying is indeed accurate. Then, every time the person exhibits that behavior, the organization will highlight it. This can make life really difficult for a person who is trying to address developmental gaps.

Think about the last time that you genuinely tried to change a behavior and develop new leadership competencies. Chances are that it was hard. What happened when you had a momentary lapse back into the "old you"? In a toxic, unforgiving culture, someone would have seized on the moment and said (probably not to your face), "Ha! See? I told you he wouldn't change!"

Cultures in which people, especially senior people, speak negatively about each other are detrimental to the environment required to develop leaders. Leaders grow best in a **compassionate and nurturing environment** that challenges them in a supportive way. Our clients sometimes object to this idea based on a misguided view that adversity is the best and indeed *only* way to build character. Some cite the U.S. Marine Corps Crucible as an example of an effective means of sorting out the good from the bad leaders. It is the final test in the training of a Marine recruit and simulates combat situations.

However, we did some research with the Marines, and the reality is almost the opposite of the "Hollywood-informed" perception. The point of the Crucible in Marine training is to build camaraderie and teamwork and to create a bonding experience that *unites the unit* thereafter. The Marines are one of the toughest organizations in the world, yet they believe in creating a nurturing environment. Speaking negatively about another Marine is unthinkable, and recklessly or even thoughtlessly damaging the reputation and therefore the leadership credibility of another Marine would be a grave matter.

One Marine we worked with at the recruiting station in Dallas, Master Sergeant Goodrich, summed up the Marine leadership philosophy beautifully when he said, "Leadership is the process of stripping yourself of being selfish; it is the antidote to the disease of 'me' in this world."

This comment was a lightbulb moment for us. It highlighted the fact that the problem with constantly speaking negatively about a colleague is *selfishness*. By dumping on a colleague, you avoid dealing with the real problem. You fail to own your part in creating the unhelpful situation. Organizational psychologists call this the *stereotyping* or *projection* defense mechanism. Professor Ben Bryant of the Institute for Management Development at Lausanne, Switzerland, gives a great example of how projection works. He tells of getting into the elevator at the office and pressing the button for the third floor. Just before the doors close, a colleague gets in and presses the button for the second floor. Ben silently thinks, "Lazy b******." Ben explains what is really happening in the elevator: he knows that he should not be taking the lift to travel up a mere two floors, but can project that antipathy onto the colleague and therefore avoid facing his own laziness.

The issue is not so much with the negativity of a single interaction but with the tendency for the momentum of the interaction to escalate and spiral out of control. One negative comment leads to and builds on the previous one, to the point where people lose a sense of perspective on the problem at hand and engage in a sort of negativity feeding frenzy. Although this can happen to an individual, it's even more likely in groups. The advent of social media such as Twitter and Facebook has brought this phenomenon into mainstream consciousness. We have seen examples of negative comments in social media that create a firestorm of negativity which quickly gets out of control and leads to real damage to innocent people's lives.

Groupshift

You may be familiar with a phenomenon called *groupthink*, in which the members of a team or group start to conform to collective perspectives on problems and solutions. Groupthink is especially likely to arise in groups that have not learned how to manage conflict in the way we described in Chapter Two. There's another, equally damaging phenomenon called *groupshift*, which is the propensity for the early ideas presented in a group to become disproportionately persuasive and carry more weight. Thus when someone in the group offers a negative opinion early on, it can sway the whole discussion. It is at this point that you can step up, exercise leadership, and reverse the conversation's direction before it gathers momentum, in the same way that our CFO client did when his team wanted to get into a "dumping" session on the law firm partner.

Momentum in a group, or even in a one-on-one discussion, is essential to making progress; otherwise, you get stuck. However, it can lead to poor outcomes when it is destructive in tone. We all need to be thoughtful in our conclusions and remain wary of being carried along by a discussion's momentum. When groups start to agree on a topic and coalesce around a problem's diagnosis and potential solution, they begin to form closer bonds. They take comfort in the fact that they are agreeing and become convinced that their argument is a good one. When this happens, groups tend to speed up in their thinking and can make potentially fatal jumps in logic that are not soundly rooted in either evidence or robust inquiry.

Try this logic puzzle: a pond has water lilies growing on it that double in size every day. After forty-eight days, the lilies have covered the pond. How many days did it take for the pond to be half covered? Most people intuitively say twenty-four days, but the answer is forty-seven! Even though you know that this is a puzzle and are therefore forewarned, you can't stop your intuitive mind from jumping to the "twenty-four" conclusion, although your rational mind was alerted to danger. Now imagine if you had done this in a room full of people who had shouted out, "Twenty-four." Would you have second-guessed yourself?

The kind of negative interactions that we described at the beginning of this chapter are not just redundant; they can spiral out of control, and if you have engaged in groupshift early on, they can lead you and your team to places and conclusions that may not be appropriate or justifiable.

Familiarity Bias

When you habitually connect two ideas, they become hardwired. One of the most common logic flaws is based on this phenomenon and is called the *familiarity bias*, which suggests that the more frequently we hear something, the more we tend to believe that it is true.[1] We confuse familiarity with veracity or accuracy. When we challenge a fact, we are more likely to test whether it resonates with us—to assess its familiarity—than to question its source. Therefore, if you habitually engage in a redundant conversation about a given topic, you are likely to lose your objectivity and come to see the discussion's conclusions as true, beyond what any evidence can support. We often find examples of this when we conduct strategic planning workshops. When clients first produce the all too familiar SWOT analysis (strengths, weaknesses, opportunities, and threats), they very often write down that their people are one of their strengths. After all, what CEO has not at some point said, "Our people are our greatest asset"? Everyone hears this so much that no one questions it. However, we have to remind our clients that your people are only a strategic strength if they are better than your competitors' people. When we ask the question, "What makes you think your people are any more professional, committed, and skilled than your main competitors' people?" we often get embarrassed silence.

Step Up

You don't have to be the group's formal leader to recognize negative momentum and exercise the kind of leadership that will reverse that momentum. And you don't have to be the senior person in any one-on-one interaction either. Here are some ways to approach it.

Identify Redundant Interactions

Most people readily accept the need to change the momentum of a clearly negative and redundant interaction, but the real challenge is to *identify when* an interaction has become redundant. Our adaptation of an idea proposed by Stephen Covey is useful for doing so. Covey made a distinction between what he called your *circle of concern* and your *circle of influence*. We add a third circle: your *circle of control* (see Figure 6.1).

- Your **circle of control** contains issues whose outcome you can directly affect.
- Your **circle of influence** contains matters whose outcome you can influence that do not fall within your direct control.

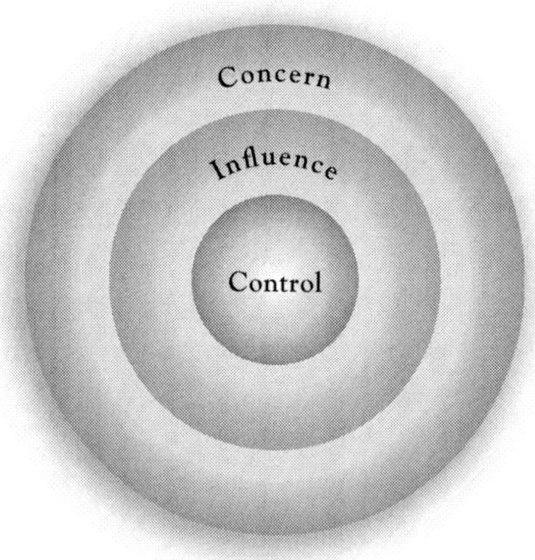

Figure 6.1 Circles of Control, Influence, and Concern
Copyright © Dynamic Results, LLC

- Your **circle of concern** contains things that affect you and over which you can exert no influence or control.

When faced with a potentially redundant conversation, we advise that you ask yourself the questions in the left-hand column of Table 6.1.

Apply ABCDE

Imagine that a man named John is always late for meetings. This bugs you, and you don't like John very much to begin with.

Table 6.1 Applying the Circles of Concern, Influence, and Control Model

Is this matter within my circle of control?	If yes:	Focus on solutions-oriented thinking and avoid restating the problem; for example, "We have established that John is often late to meetings. What can we do to help him be on time?"
	If no:	Move to the circle-of-influence question.
Is this matter within my circle of influence?	If yes:	Ask, "Is the person I need to influence in the conversation with me?" If yes: Focus on getting to a win-win solution. If no: Focus on how you are going to have the conversation in which you try to exert influence; for example, "We can't control this matter ourselves, but I think we all know who makes this decision. Who has the best relationship with that decision maker, and are you willing to discuss this with that person to see if we can get support?"
	If no:	Move to the circle-of-concern question.

(Continued)

Table 6.1 (*Continued*)

Is this matter within my circle of concern?	If yes:	Try to estimate the impact of changes in key external uncontrollable variables and develop contingency plans to address those changes. Avoid focusing on the potential problem and get on with your business, knowing that you have a mitigation plan ready. For example, you might say, "I also feel frustrated by what is happening, and I think we have exhausted all our resources trying to figure out what we can do about it. It seems that this is out of our control, and we should move on to other topics that we *can* control or influence."
	If no:	You are almost certainly having a redundant conversation! Enjoy it if it is fun, but be conscious of the burn rate. The topic would probably be best left for a conversation over a glass of good wine sometime.

Rather quickly, you stop seeing John's being late and your not liking John as two ideas. They actually become one idea in your mind. This is a situation where you can apply the ABCDE principle. The letters stand for

Activating event

Belief

Conclusion

Dispute

Evidence

The activating event (A) was that John was late, and the conclusion (C) is that you don't like John. Now we want you to focus on the B part: the belief. What is it that you have to believe in order to make the conclusion you have reached plausible? Typically this belief has become unconscious, as the activating event and the conclusion have become fused into one idea in your mind.

You have to believe that John is lazy, disrespectful, doesn't like you, and so on. Your conclusion would not stand up if John was very busy, had to drop his kids to school on the mornings of your meetings, or was incapable of telling time. Exposing the underlying belief will often be enough to help you recognize that you are jumping to conclusions. Now come the D and E parts: dispute the belief, ask what else might explain the behavior, and then look for evidence to confirm the other alternatives.

A client of ours had this very problem, and she worked through the thought process for her initial read of the situation using the ABCDE method to come up with an alternative hypothesis to test.

Initial Read

Activating event	John is consistently late for my meetings.
Belief	John does not respect my time and feels that it's OK to be late.
Conclusion	John is lazy and not a team player. I need to do something about the "John problem."
Dispute/ debate	He is usually late, but does seem well prepared when he eventually shows up. He has never given any other signs of disrespect. Could there be some other reason why he is late?

Evidence	He is leading a project that I am very focused on, and I gave him a hard time at the first meeting because he hadn't gotten his facts straight and was missing a key input from one of the field sales teams. He seems a bit "twitchy" in the meetings and looks quite defensive.

An alternative belief she could hold was that John was late because he waited until the last minute to get all of the latest data from the field in order to be fully prepared in the meetings. When she substituted this belief, she came to a different conclusion: that she made John nervous and that this anxiety was affecting his performance.

"I make John nervous" was one possible alternative explanation for what was going on. The client then looked for evidence that could either confirm or deny her alternative explanation. As it happens, she was pretty much spot-on in her assessment of the true reason why John was being late. She was then able to remedy his nervousness about her, help him develop a stronger rapport with the guys in the field, and get his data in.

Ask, "What Would It Take?"

Think about the last time you engaged in a negative conversation about a colleague's behavior. Take a few moments right now to ask yourself honestly:

- Are there ways in which I either catalyzed or facilitated the very behavior that we are complaining about?
- Did I collude in the negative conversation in order to feel connected with the group or the individual leading the conversation?

- What would it take for me to be the one to stand up and interrupt this flow the next time it happens?

State It Once

Name a problem if a problem exists, and do so in a productive and constructive way. You might need to address somebody's behavior, or simply a process. But it is never a good idea to just leave it alone and not mention it. By stating it once, you call attention to the problem; you put it on the table where people can look at it and acknowledge its existence.

If you then start to repeat the problem or have a redundant discussion about a person's shortcoming, you know you're starting to damage his reputation and demean him—and not doing anything to solve the problem. After you state a problem once in a productive and constructive way, the best thing to do is change the conversation's momentum, shifting from a focus on the problem and toward a focus on the solution.[2]

Let's say that a colleague named Bill habitually agreed to take on tasks and then failed to follow through, a fact that was bothering both you and another colleague. That colleague might say, "You know, Bill often agrees to take on a task and then doesn't follow through. That's causing problems for me."

This is when your leadership moment happens. Suppose that instead of responding, "Yeah, you're right. Bill does that often, and it drives me crazy too," you say, "You're right; Bill does do that. What do you think might be the cause?" or "You're right; is there anything going on in his personal life that could be the cause?" or "What do you think is the root cause of that tendency—and what can we do to help him?"

The leaders in an organization are the people who *habitually move* from stating problems to finding solutions. Whenever they sense that negative momentum is building, they immediately convert it to a solution-oriented dialogue. Those leaders can come from *any* position on an organization chart; title doesn't matter.

Choose Your Thoughts

We've already noted that habitually speaking ill about a colleague can cement his or her reputation. People also tend to confirm ideas and perceptions about individuals, organizations, situations, and specific meetings in a way that may be difficult to undo even within their own minds.

Imagine that there is a regularly occurring weekly meeting that you really don't like attending. The first diagram (Figure 6.2) shows what can easily happen if you entertain the thought, "I hate that weekly meeting." You can launch yourself on a negative path that drives your mood, your behavior, and your self-image—all of which probably guarantee that you will continue to hate the weekly meeting.

Contrast that scenario with the one illustrated in Figure 6.3. Here you resolve to do something to improve the meeting. This stimulates a completely different path through a positive mood, behavior, and self-image.

Just as you can reverse negative momentum in one-on-one conversations and in the meetings you attend, you can also reverse your own negative momentum by choosing thoughts that start a positive cycle.

Summary of Key Learnings in Chapter Six

- Negative, redundant discussions are horrible wasters of time and resources.
- You cause someone reputational damage when you speak negatively about her—which may endure even after she has changed her behavior.

Figure 6.2 Negative Thought Cycle
Copyright © Dynamic Results, LLC

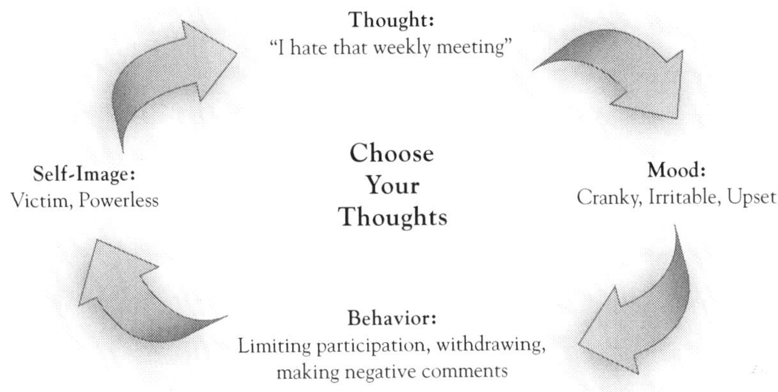

Figure 6.3 Positive Thought Cycle
Copyright © Dynamic Results, LLC

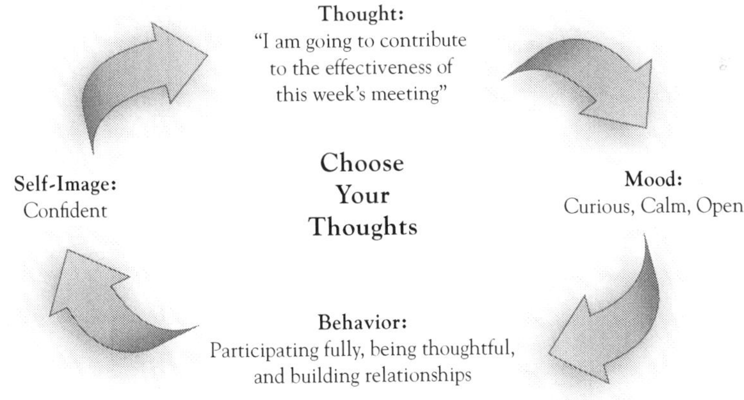

- Momentum in a group or even in a one-one-one discussion is essential to making progress; otherwise, you get stuck. However, it can lead to poor outcomes when it is destructive in tone.
- If you habitually engage in redundant conversations, you are likely to lose your objectivity. You come to see the conclusions of the discussions as true, beyond what any evidence can support.
- Human energy and creativity are like the fuel you put in a car or airplane. Each tank is a limited resource and should be expended on moving "forward." Spinning around in circles is a waste of precious resources. Leaders habitually move quickly from stating problems to finding solutions.

Your Next Steps to Step Up and Reverse the Momentum of Negative Interactions

- Identify a meeting or interaction where you or others habitually dump on a colleague or coworker. Resolve to be the person who steps up the next time to move the group to solution mode. Remember to allow for a venting session later (*not* during company time).
- Keep the burn rate displayed at meetings and conferences—at least until everyone is aware of how much time redundant conversations can waste and begins to use time more productively.
- Use the "circles of control, influence, and concern" approach at your next team meeting or one-on-one session. Whenever you are getting into a discussion about a topic that lies within your circle of concern, remind the group of the burn rate and encourage it to move on.
- Apply the ABCDE tool to a situation you're facing right now. Identify an alternative explanation and genuinely look

for evidence that suggests that this alternative explanation holds water.

- Make "State It Once" a group or even organization-wide mantra.
- Print out your emails from the past two weeks. Color code each email: green = circle of control; yellow = circle of influence; red = circle of concern. Now step back for an overview of how you are spending your time. If you see a lot of red, consider using this process to "triage" all future emails.

Step Up Link

Video of the authors speaking about managing pessimists with the "State It Once" approach

Conclusion
Create Emotional Safety

A leader is best when people barely know he exists,
when his work is done, his aim fulfilled, they
will say: we did it ourselves.
—*Lao Tzu*

Our Promise

In our conclusion, we will discuss the concept of *emotional safety* and show you how to become your organization's Director of Emotional Safety. In this role, you'll be the person who is given a clean and accurate read of situations; the one who hears first, not last, when there is a problem; and the one who operates with good rather than bad intelligence. You will make people feel safe, appreciated, and perhaps even rewarded for bringing you bad news. The tools and techniques in this chapter can help you become the best-informed person in the room, one who is able to wield power wisely. There are those to whom people do not want to bring bad news, and those to whom people feel encouraged to bring bad news. The latter group is better informed. We will show you how to be in that group.

Getting Good Intel

An ambitious young executive, let's call him Kiat, with whom we worked was making a real name for himself in a Fortune 100 company. He had a great track record, driven mainly by his brilliant mind. Unfortunately, he also had a huge temper—which caused him to learn about emotional safety the hard way. The people who worked for him were split into two camps. Some of them loved working for him (but didn't love *him*) and sought to be carried along by his success. The rest, about 75 percent, either feared or hated him. He felt that people should do things because he told them to; after all, he reasoned, he was the boss.

This is an outdated approach to leadership. As recently as the beginning of this century, people were still looking to join one company and stay there twenty years in pursuit of a pension. Today, few people plan to spend more than five years in a single job. We live in a more connected, collaborative world, and the dated command-and-control style lowers engagement and encourages people to look for other jobs (and withhold information).

Kiat's company was expanding and had targeted one Southeast Asian country as the key to unlocking the entire region. The launch was the highest-profile plank of the company's strategic plan for that year. His team worked hard on the launch, but hit a major snag: the regulatory approval they needed was delayed and buried in layers of bureaucracy.

They realized the problem, but continued to push for the proposal and lobby for government approval. They spent a significant amount of hours and dollars in what turned out to be a fruitless pursuit. It took the team nearly four months to find the "right moment" to approach Kiat—that is, when they felt that he was in a good enough mood to raise the issue with him. Within weeks of getting the bad news, he saw that the proposed strategy needed to be changed, and switched focus to target a different country as the launch market.

Although the strategy worked out reasonably well in the end, our client struggled to understand the huge waste of time and money his company had endured because people were too afraid of him to admit defeat. He didn't see himself as a bad person and certainly did not want others to fear him; but it was only when he confronted his disdain for the idea of being the Director of Emotional Safety that he saw how destructive his approach had been. He caught himself saying, "This emotional safety stuff is a bunch of crap; people should just say what they mean." As soon as the words came out of his mouth, Kiat realized why his people couldn't speak their minds to him—and he suddenly understood how he might make others feel.

The critical importance of making others feel emotionally and psychologically safe has been recognized in a number of environments—some even surprising. For example, the FBI Academy has recently been focusing on the emotional intelligence competencies of high-performing agents. Our colleague Dr. Timothy Turner—a retired FBI agent and program manager for FBI leadership development at the FBI Academy—said that empathy can have the most impact on an agent's effectiveness. Those agents who can build relationships with others—suspects, other agencies, sources, and colleagues—and make them feel safe are the most effective.

Many people find this ideal a little difficult to reconcile with the macho corporate world. We like the way Eric Greitens, former U.S. Navy Seal and Rhodes Scholar, expressed the importance of emotional safety in his book *The Heart and the Fist*: "The world's best interrogators proceed not by fear and intimidation, but by establishing rapport with their prisoners and learning from them over time. . . . [T]he world's most effective interrogators, from World War II to the present day, are men who use their intelligence to establish rapport and gain information."[1]

The higher you are on the organization chart, the more power you wield. You make higher-leverage and potentially riskier decisions. You receive an ever-growing *quantity* of information; but at a time when you need good-quality data, there's a chance that you may be suffering from an **information integrity problem**. Unless you make it safe for people to bring you bad news and to honestly discuss problems and failures, you'll get information that's distorted by people's fear of your reactions, especially if the news is about you. Bad news is suppressed until it *has* to be shared, and good news is overplayed.

What's more worrisome is that your people know that you love to hear evidence that your decisions are working out well. This problem is the hardest to recognize, because those around you have a vested interest in your believing that you are well informed. You may delude yourself about the quality of your data, and there may be people around you who want to keep you in that deluded state. We believe that when someone high up who makes big decisions fails to create emotional safety, he or she is not only one of the most powerful people in the organization but also one of the most dangerous. The principle applies at any level. Whatever your place on the org chart, people are relying on you to be informed about your function. A lack of emotional safety puts you in danger of making decisions in an information vacuum.

We have saved our discussion about emotional safety until the end of this book because it is a capstone; it brings together the ideas we have already shared. If you have been practicing the skills explained in the previous six chapters, you can now

- Use negative emotion wisely (Chapter One)
- Avoid terminal politeness (Chapter Two)

- Be more decisive (Chapter Three)
- Be more aware of your own need to change (Chapter Four)
- Leverage the wisdom of pessimists (Chapter Five)
- Reverse the momentum of negative interactions (Chapter Six)

However, you won't be successful unless you can enact these behaviors in a way that is emotionally safe for others as well.

It Isn't All About You

Many people achieve leadership positions, especially in hierarchical organizations, through their strong individual contributions and achievement orientation. However, you derive leadership success not through your own actions but through the actions of others.[2] This becomes more and more true as you work your way up the organization chart. This is the challenge that management researchers refer to as the *paradox of leadership*: the very qualities that get people promoted to leadership positions often prevent them from allowing others to shine.

The job of the Director of Emotional Safety is to create a context or environment that encourages others to produce excellent work. For instance, when faced with a choice about whether or not to display your anger, ask, "How will the other person feel or react if I show my anger now?" If it would produce a desired effect in the other person, go ahead and show it; if not, don't. Business management expert Edward Deming is reputed to have said, "Only say it if it serves," meaning that you should make a comment only if it will produce the result that you want. Making yourself feel better temporarily is probably not a sufficient reason. A Director of Emotional Safety understands that exercising leadership is not about himself or herself.

This idea is at the heart of our understanding of true leadership: it requires a genuine focus on others and less of a focus on yourself. Leadership calls on your ability to influence others to exercise the free choice to follow you. Imagine that the people who work for you are given a secret ballot in which they can choose who should be their boss. How many of them would pick you?

In the past, people assumed that confident, assertive, type A personalities made the best leaders. But the emerging knowledge-driven economy will require a different type. Management experts now recognize the value of what has come to be known as *post heroic leadership*—getting beyond the "leader as hero" concept and seeing leadership as a phenomenon that leader and follower cocreate, with each playing equally important parts. Among its other effects, this dynamic has cracked the glass ceiling and paved the way for more women in leadership roles.[3]

We support the need to tear down the outdated type A leadership stereotype. Organizations must start recruiting, developing, rewarding, retaining, and promoting leaders who have this more current and integrated approach.

You can validate this yourself by thinking about your own interactions with leaders. Try to remember the person who got the best out of you, for whom you did your best work. Was he or she the smartest, the toughest, the most supportive? People tend to give different answers depending on the type of leadership to which they respond best. However, there is one thing that the people who bring out the best in us have in common: they have our best interests at heart. This is perhaps best captured in an adage attributed to Theodore Roosevelt: "People don't care how much you know until they know how much you care."

Leaders who make a real, human, genuine connection with us prompt us to try harder, work smarter, and give more. How many of the people who report to you now would see you in the same light as you see the person who got the best out of *you*? Are you being this type of leader to your people?

We know what you might be thinking: "Get real—I'm not here to make friends. I'm here to do a good professional job, make some money, and then go home to my real family." We understand and respect that perspective. We aren't advocating that you create emotional safety for others because it "feels good." We support this approach because it is a smarter and more effective way to *run your organization*. In short, in the words of one of our clients, "This sh*t works!"

You may be a humanist and do it because you care about how other people feel; you may do it because you are a capitalist with an almost exclusive focus on driving profit and performance. Either way, creating emotional safety for others helps you remain informed and achieve your goals in a sustainable way.

We're struck by the clarity with which military leaders make the distinction between the legal authority to command based on one's position on the org chart and the moral authority to lead, which has nothing to do with rank and is all about the depth of connection with one's team. If your team members don't respect and trust you, then what can you really command them to do? At most, they'll comply with the letter of their job descriptions. Is that adequate for dealing with the challenges you are facing now? If you can create emotional safety for others, you create the opportunity to develop the real human connections with them that will form the foundation of your leadership power. Eric Shinseki, former Army chief of staff, summed this up brilliantly when he said, "Without leadership, command is a hollow experience, a vacuum often filled with mistrust and arrogance."[4]

Why It Works

The story at the beginning of this conclusion about the young executive whose team withheld important information from him illustrates two reasons that creating emotional safety is a smart thing to do. The first is that the quality of your information deteriorates when people don't feel safe talking to you. If you have a boss you don't fully trust—someone who has a habit of shooting the messenger—what are the odds that you'll always tell him the full story? Even if you do, how much *extra* time and resources do you put into making sure you have your facts right—and how long do you spend on getting the message pitched just right? Most people don't always volunteer the full story to this kind of person, always double-check their facts, and are very careful about how they present the message. This is what your people are doing whenever they have to deliver a tricky message, if they don't trust you.

Making people fearful motivates them to avoid your displeasure—which can create a blind side for you. Bad stuff happens all the time. People make mistakes, product launches fail, and software implementations run over budget. When people fear your response, they will do almost anything to keep that kind of information from you for as long as possible. An environment where people cover up mistakes and departments play the blame game is very dangerous.

Others might also be motivated to bring you information that flatters your previous decision-making record, only delivering a "sanitized" version of events. They gloss over failures from which you could learn, which only makes you likely to repeat them in some form. They overplay or spin successes. Problems that you could have helped to solve had you been brought into the loop soon enough will fester until they are so big that they can no longer be covered up—and at that point, even you can't fix them. Every time you see a budget number, you will experience a nagging feeling that there is some padding built in that you are not being told about. You will be presented with problems only after everyone else in the organization has had a go at fixing them and failed.

The second reason that creating emotional safety is valuable is that when you *don't* operate as the Director of Emotional Safety, you run the risk that your people will pursue goals beyond the point where the pursuit continues to make good sense. This phenomenon is referred to as *destructive goal pursuit*; the term is based on an analysis of the climbing disaster that occurred on Mount Everest, which we discussed in Chapter Four.[5] Five climbers were killed because they refused to honor their turnaround time, abandon their attempt to reach the summit, and turn back. Abandoning a clear and compelling goal is a very risky and emotionally fraught decision. When you operate as the Director of Emotional Safety, you make your people more comfortable in facing up to these decisions quickly and decisively. They won't feel as though they have to wait for the "right time" to gain your attention.

One of the first things we do when we work with clients is take a hard look at their list of outstanding projects. We very often find a long list of initiatives, some of which have been on the books for a long time. This is very often a sign of destructive goal pursuit. Often as many as 50 *percent* of those projects should be killed off, but no one wants to be the one to raise this with the CEO, especially if it's a project he's championed. But every project you choose to keep alive represents one new project that you cannot launch. To ensure that you are prioritizing wisely, you must have access to the best and most honest internal assessments.

There is a third reason that creating emotional safety makes sense: people simply don't grow in a fearful environment. In fact, people working under conditions of fear or stress fall back on what is called *heuristic* reasoning: relying solely on experience and failing to use their intellect to solve new problems. It might be because stress impairs explicit memory, which is used to rationally deal with a problem, and enhances implicit memory, which fires up emotionally laden experience-based rules of thumb.[6] If you manage smart people in a way that makes them fearful, you rob them—as well as yourself and the organization—of the intelligence you hired them for in the first place.

When you don't make the environment safe for people, either through an unwise display of anger or by attacking someone, you guarantee that they will not look to you for guidance in difficult situations. You also create a situation where team members suppress, sanitize, or spin data that may show your team in a bad light. Rather than focusing on solutions, your team members become black belts in offering sophisticated reasons for failure. And if your team is focused on excuses, they are not thinking about solutions.

Two Keys

Being the Director of Emotional Safety is not always about making people feel good. We don't want you to see this role as a kind of organizational Santa Claus to whom people turn for free hugs when they are feeling down or anxious. There are two key principles to keep in mind as you assume the role.

The first is that **you must get the balance right between supporting and challenging your people**, between nurturing them and holding them to account for their mistakes and missteps, and between creating an organizational climate that resembles a country club and creating one that resembles a coal mine.

Turner, whom we referenced earlier, talks about getting the balance right when he describes the need for assertiveness in FBI agents, which often involves a display of negative emotion. When agents are too assertive, they may abuse force. But when they suppress anger and lack assertiveness, they may become targets for exploitation or attack. People perform best when they strike a balance between their competence to do their work and the level of challenge in that work.[7] When they're not challenged enough, they become bored. Highly intelligent, bored individuals can be very disruptive—just ask any kindergarten teacher.

One element of finding balance is providing both clarity about what failure looks like and a significant level of emotional discomfort with failure.[8] As an effective Director of Emotional Safety, you can create a high-performance team around you whether you are the formal team leader or not. If you use the tools and techniques in this book, you will no longer have to be tough on your team's mistakes; they will do that for themselves. When your people feel bad about making a mistake, you have to allow them to feel bad. Don't rush in to rescue them, and don't add your own anger to the mix. When people don't recognize their mistakes and need a judicious boot in their rear end, it is OK for them to experience a bit of your anger or frustration. Just make sure that you, not your anger, are in control. General Stanley McChrystal of the U.S. Army described this as the ability to allow people to fail without making them feel like a failure.[9]

There are times when you may display negative emotion in an unproductive way, when you have to be decisive, when you have to curtail debate and insist on following your own course of action. People around you will see that these occasional forceful actions are driven by external circumstance, that even though you would *like* to be more supportive and collaborative, you simply don't have the time or space. So long as this is not your default style, most people can accept the need for you to drive through an issue in this way. Again, you need to achieve a balance between forceful action and supportiveness.

The second principle is that **making it safe for people to be honest with you frees them to be vulnerable around you** (see Figure C.1). When they are, reciprocate. Being vulnerable with

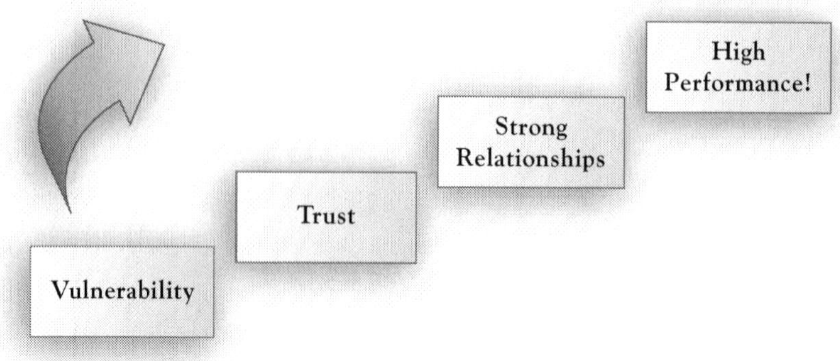

Figure C.1 The Steps to High Performance
Copyright © Dynamic Results, LLC

someone is crucial to building trust, and trust is the foundation of relationships.

A female senior executive in a male-dominated organization had decided to suppress all indications of both positive and negative emotion as well as her nurturing side, in an attempt to fit in with her "macho" company. No one knew anything about her life outside work, and no one could read her emotions. While this enigmatic persona provided endless hours of idle speculation for the junior staffers around the watercooler, the executive's lack of emotional honesty inhibited her from connecting with her colleagues. It severely impaired her influence at the board room table.

This highly capable executive's inability to be vulnerable had caused her to derail in several other positions. She never got angry or upset, but she never seemed pleased or happy either. Although none of her colleagues ever had anything specifically negative to say about her, people could not read her, so they didn't trust her.

Being the Director of Emotional Safety is about finding the right balance between displaying too much and too little emotion. As this executive grew more open and honest about her feelings, people began to warm to her. Soon she found that her ability to lead, inspire, motivate, and influence—as the Director of Emotional Safety—was significantly amplified and was much more effective than her ability when she relied on her technical expertise alone.

Do you trust people enough, or are you wary until you know people better? As a leader, you have to make the first move. Withholding trust until people have demonstrated competence is not *trust*; you don't have to trust someone who has already proven his or her worth.

In high-risk, potentially destructive moments, you have to not only risk trusting others but also demonstrate that *you* are trustworthy. The ability to be authentically yourself is critical to building a trusting relationship with others; and in order to be authentically yourself, you have to be able to display all of your emotions, even the dark ones, in a healthy and productive way. As is true of other skills, effectively expressing your emotions will become easier the more you do it. Practice displaying negative emotion in a healthy way, so that you have the option of doing so when you need people to read you accurately and not just feel the heat of your negative emotion.

Breathing-In Moments

Imagine that you are approaching your boss's office with bad news. Those moments will be either "breathing-in" or "breathing-out" moments, depending on your past experiences with your boss. During a breathing-in moment, you think something like, "Oh, damn. I have this problem, and I have to go talk to him, and he fired the last two people who brought him bad news." A breathing-out moment allows you to think, "I've got this problem, but he is a good guy to bring a problem to. He doesn't kill the messenger, and he's very solutions focused." If people who are in relationship with you are experiencing a lot of breathing-in moments, they're likely to withhold information—keeping you in an information vacuum. The less emotional safety you create, the more power you surrender.

Directors of emotional safety create more breathing-out moments for other people. They accomplish this by

- Taking advantage of the leadership moments described in previous chapters
- Listening without defending
- Speaking without offending

. . . and doing all three consistently.

Listening without defending is especially difficult. If you were to receive constructive criticism, would you be more likely to respond, "Well, you are the only one saying that, so it can't be true," or "Thanks for telling me how you feel and what your experience is. I'm going to go look into that because that is not the experience I want you to have." As we've mentioned elsewhere, other people will interact with you based on what they think of you—not on what *you* believe they should think. Understanding what they think of you will help you predict how they will interact with you in the future, so encourage constructive criticism and let others know that you appreciate them for offering it.

This tendency also applies to speaking without offending. What seems inoffensive to you may very well be offensive to someone else. For example, a new leader came to a company with a long-term strategic goal of causing positive attrition, assessing competence and pushing out people who he felt shouldn't be there. He managed to alienate the entire executive team on his first morning by saying, "There is no question that I'm the right person for this job, because the board of directors had multiple candidates when they picked me. There are a lot of questions about your capabilities because, right now, you guys suck." Yes, he really said this. This is obviously an egregious example; sometimes you can cause offense even through what you don't say.

In one of Colm's first leadership roles, he took over a team of four accountants. Three of the team members were seen as high potential, and Colm was advised to meet with them to discuss their role and his vision for the team going forward. The fourth accountant was a woman who was about to go on maternity leave. The senior director in the company suggested that she probably would not come back to work in the long term and didn't seem all that motivated. Whereas he met with the first three accountants within two days, Colm didn't speak with the fourth until two weeks after he started the new role, and, as you can probably guess, she was highly (and justifiably) offended. Luckily Colm made a fulsome apology; she later did in fact return to work, and turned out to be a star performer.

The Right Balance

Your ability to create emotional safety will prompt people to be open and honest with you about your ideas and suggestions and their own performance. Management consultant Patrick Lencioni provides a great illustration of the distorting effect that power can have on information integrity. A CEO brought the 360-degree feedback he received to his management team and said, "This feedback says that I'm a bad listener; do you guys feel that I'm a bad listener?"

To which all the team members mumbled something like, "No, boss, you're a good listener."

The CEO then said something like, "It also says I can be abrupt with people. Is that true?"

While looking to each other and then at the conference room table, they mumbled something like, "Um . . . I don't think so; well, not with me anyway."

If the company ran the 360-degree assessment in six months' time, the results would no longer say that the CEO was a bad listener or abrupt. But what has he improved? Did the CEO change his behavior? Has he in fact become a better listener? No; the feedback has become distorted. The team members, who don't want another mortifying inquisition from the CEO, simply decided to *tell him what he wanted to hear*.

The real information that you will receive—particularly about your own performance—as a Director of Emotional Safety is the only known antidote to the "structurally induced narcissism" that accompanies positions of power.[10] You will see issues and opportunities more clearly and quickly; people will bring ideas and suggestions to you more readily. You will be the first, not the last, to know when problems arise, and you can decide whether to intervene or not. You will stop wasting time in second-guessing the reports you receive, as you know that people are comfortable being honest with you. Remember the leader who inspired you and whom you reflected on at the start of this chapter? Becoming the Director of Emotional Safety will allow you to have the impact on others that he or she had on you.

Great leaders create an atmosphere characterized by genuine personal connection and warmth, one where the cold light of intellect is balanced with a human touch. We describe the great leaders with whom we've worked as people we love and respect, both parts being equally important. How many of your staff, past or present, would say that they love and respect you? Real personal connections are becoming increasingly rare in our fast-paced, pressurized business world.

A Director of Emotional Safety knows how to achieve the right balance between rationality and warmth. Your organization will go a long way toward creating an environment free from politics and gaming, one in which employees feel comfortable discussing real issues openly and honestly. People will be free to admit mistakes and learn real lessons as a result of reviewing both failures and successes.

Recognize the Signs

Recognizing when you are at risk of creating an emotionally unsafe environment requires that you really tune in to what others are saying—and, just as important, *not* saying—and reflect on how you've contributed to that environment. Specifically, learning how to spot signs of anxiety in others will help you identify when you need to be especially mindful of how you are affecting them.

We like to use the example of colors and emotions. Let's say that anger = red, happiness = blue, relief = green, and so forth. If you were standing at a boarding gate and had your emotional x-ray goggles on, you would see a rainbow of colors when a delay was announced. Most people would turn a shade of red; others might show relief (green) that they have "more time to work" or read or stay on the phone. The same is true in meetings. It is crucially important to be in touch with how other people in the meeting feel before you do a deep dive into data. We advise our clients to ask the following types of questions:

- Do the words match the music? This requires you to compare the *content* of what is being said to the *tone* in which it is said. For example, if someone is making a minor point but investing a lot of energy (maybe even anger) in it, he or she obviously cares deeply about it.

- Is someone speaking in an uncharacteristic manner—faster or louder than usual?
- Is someone displaying irritation for no apparent reason?
- Are people showing physical signs of discomfort, such as wringing their hands, fiddling with pens, or "coloring up," especially at the neck?
- Are people ganging up on anyone whom you criticize—a form of scapegoating?

You can ask a clarifying question, such as, "I might be off base here, but you seem a little worried about this. Is there anything I can do to support you?" You should also be very mindful of your own energy level: slow down, speak calmly, try to sit with the group rather than adopt a confrontational stance, get down to eye level with them. Though we hope it goes without saying, you cannot achieve this type of sensitivity to others via email. You have to go and speak with people to pick up on the human dynamics in any interaction.

Take a Time-Out (for Yourself)

Creating emotional safety for others isn't easy when you become increasingly frustrated or otherwise emotionally charged during an interaction with them. When you feel you cannot control yourself, and think that it is because of how the other person is behaving, we recommend that you say something like, "The discussion we are having right now is starting to upset me, and I don't feel that I can discuss this objectively right now. That's not fair to you, so my request is that we discuss this tomorrow when I will be in a more balanced and objective state of mind."

This doesn't necessarily mean that the other person isn't completely crazy; indeed, perhaps he or she is and or is acting that way. But you can control only your own behavior, so impose a "time-out" if need be and return to the discussion at a time when you are likely to be proud of what you say. It's during the emotionally charged moments when we don't take the time-out that we frequently do and say things that we later regret—and we know in hindsight that we were capable of doing much better than we did.

During your time-out, before you reconvene, ask yourself the following questions:

- On days when I'm at my personal best, how would I approach this discussion?
- If the roles were reversed, how would I want this person to approach me? What should the person look and sound like?

These questions prompt you to think about your average performance (mood, demeanor, approach) versus *your personal best*. Imagine how you might improve your situation and experience at work and at home if you could raise your average even a little closer to your best.

One especially thought-provoking question we like to ask ourselves in critical moments of choice is "Which decision will I feel proud of when I'm ninety years old?"

Prioritize

We've already discussed how destructive goal pursuit can get in the way of appropriate prioritization. The idea that you will "get it all done" is a fallacy. You are not getting it all done now, and you never will. Admitting this and helping yourself and others "down-select" is a crucial way to lead when you are part of a team. We encourage clients to use down-selection criteria such as "impact" (What would change if this was done?) and "achievability" (Can it be done?). We showed you the Prioritization Filter in Chapter Three and have seen our clients work with that model effectively when they need to down-select their priorities.

We advise our clients to **proactively kill projects** on a regular basis and to set clear milestones and stick with them. When a project is heading off track, you must seriously question whether you wouldn't be better off redirecting the organizational resources that would be required to get it back on track.

Focus on Solutions Rather Than Mistakes

Mistakes are potential leadership moments for you as the Director of Emotional Safety. How you react in these risky and potentially destructive moments will characterize and define both your leadership and your reputation. Focusing on the solution and on the learning gained from the mistake develops the people around you and contributes to a speedy solution.

When you are notified of a mistake, ask yourself, "What is the best way to respond here? Is there a learning opportunity, or was this a result of laziness or recklessness? Does this issue represent a contravention of a key organizational value? What is the long-term potential of this person to my team? Is the incident more or less important than the relationship?"

Summary of Key Learnings in the Conclusion

- If you are high on the organization chart and making big decisions, operating without creating emotional safety for others makes you not only one of the most powerful people in the organization but also one of the most dangerous.

- The job of the Director of Emotional Safety is to create the context or environment in which others can produce excellent work.
- There are three reasons for assuming the role of Director of Emotional Safety: the quality of your information deteriorates when people don't feel safe around you; your people may pursue goals beyond the point where the pursuit continues to make good sense; and people do not grow in a fearful environment.
- The first principle of success as the Director of Emotional Safety is to strike the right balance between supporting and challenging your people. The second is to make it safe for people to be honest with you, and for you to reciprocate. Being vulnerable with someone is crucial to building trust.
- Successful Directors of Emotional Safety take advantage of the leadership moments described in previous chapters, listen without defending, speak without offending, take time out for themselves, balance rationality and warmth, prioritize, focus on solutions, and create breathing-out moments. They do all of these things consistently and recognize when they are *not* doing them.

Your Next Steps to Step Up and Create Emotional Safety

- Honestly assess how often you get bad news from people and how "prepared" or "cleaned up" it seems.
- Determine your own feelings about emotion in the workplace, and see how these might be affecting your interactions. Do you feel that showing emotion would be perceived as a weakness? If so, you probably aren't creating the type of emotional safety that generates good intel. Make a commitment to do one thing this week to start creating emotional safety for your team.

- Think about how the people you'd label as your "best leaders" made *you* feel. Write down three things they did or said and implement one of these each week for the next three weeks.
- Make it a group goal to kill some projects in order to make room for better ones. Have a "wake" for the projects you are going to kill off. Codify the lessons you learned from the projects and put in place procedures to ensure that these projects are not maintained "under the radar."
- Create a policy for initiating a new project: you must ask what project should make way to create space for it.
- During your next few interactions and/or when employees approach you, make a concerted effort to decipher whether it's a breathing-in or breathing-out moment for them.
- Following your interaction, conduct a post-mortem and ask your employee, "How did you feel bringing this to me? How do you feel since you brought it to me?

Step Up Link

To stay in touch with us and always receive the latest strategies and revisions to our methods, please scan here and subscribe to our complimentary monthly thought leadership blog, the *Dynamic Perspective*.

An invitation to subscribe to our newsletter

Next Steps

Use our three-minute videos to start your meetings. You will find them at http://www.dynamicresults.com/read/insight-from-our-experts/.

Use one of the videos as a conversation starter for a particular leadership topic.

Take our eSchool Journey to Step Up leadership at every level of your organization, from Winning With Accountability™ to Emotional Safety®:

- Drive Accountability (Without Leaving Dead Bodies in the Road)
- Practice Emotional Safety®

Follow us on LinkedIn for ongoing ideas and discussions with our internal experts as well as with our clients: https://www.linkedin.com/company/977221

https://www.linkedin.com/in/henryevansdynamicresults/

Hire us to consult for your company to drive accountability, ignite leadership at every level of your organization, create and implement your business strategy, and assess and develop individual leaders as well as intact leadership teams. Have us keynote your next conference or meeting.

Use the QR codes embedded at the end of each chapter for complimentary resources.

Follow us on Twitter for current ideas, reminders, and updates: @HenryJEvans

Remember that you can lead in the moments that matter!

Notes

Introduction

1. Langer, E. J. *Mindfulness*. New York: Perseus Books, 1989.
2. Kouzes, J., and Posner, L. *The Leadership Challenge*. (5th ed.) San Francisco: Jossey-Bass.

Chapter 1

1. Ohanian, A. "How to Turn Failure into Fuel." *USA Today*, Oct. 18, 2013. http://www.usatoday.com/story/opinion/2013/10/17/millennials-ohanion-reddit-column/3004033/.
2. Goleman, D. *Emotional Intelligence*. New York: Bantam Books, 1995.
3. Gaffney, M. *Flourishing*. Dublin: Penguin, 2011.
4. Ekman, P. *Emotions Revealed: Understanding Faces and Feelings*. London: Orion Books, 2004.
5. May, G. H. "Structural Brain Alterations Following 5 Days of Interventions: Dynamic Aspects of Neuroplasticity." *Cerebral Cortex*, Jan. 2007, pp. 205–210.

Chapter 2

1. Peterson, R. S., and Behfar, K. J. "The Dynamic Relationship Between Performance Feedback, Trust, and Conflict in Groups: A Longitudinal Study." *Organizational Behavior and Human Decision Processes*, 2003, 92(1–2), 102–112.
2. Hill, L. A., Travaglini, M., Brandeau, G., and Stecker, E. "Unlocking the Slices of Genius in Your Organization: Leading for Innovation."

In N. Nohria and R. Khurana (eds.), *Handbook of Leadership Theory and Practice*. Boston: Harvard Business School Publishing, 2010.

3. Quoted in Dumaine, B. "Mr. Learning Organization: Peter Senge's Goal Is Merely to Change the World by Helping People Change Deeply. His Ideas Are Paying Off at Companies Like Ford and Federal Express." *Fortune*, October 17, 1994. http://money.cnn.com/magazines/fortune/fortune_archive/1994/10/17/79843/index.htm.
4. Goleman, D. *Emotional Intelligence*. New York: Bantam Books, 1995.
5. Siegel, D. J. *The Developing Mind: Toward a Neurobiology of Interpersonal Experience*. New York: Guilford Press, 1999.
6. Knight, S. *NLP at Work*. London: Nicholas Brealey, 2009.
7. Keller, T. "Images of the Familiar: Individual Differences and Implicit Leadership Theories." *Leadership Quarterly*, Winter 1999, pp. 589–607.
8. Ehrhart, M., and Klein K. "Predicting Followers' Preferences for Charismatic Leadership: The Influence of Follower Values and Personality." *Leadership Quarterly*, Summer 2001, pp. 153–179.
9. Bell, S. "Deep Level Composition Variables as Predictors of Team Performance: A Meta-Analysis." *Journal of Applied Psychology*, May 2007, 92(3), 595–615.
10. Eden, D. "Leadership and Expectations: Pygmalion Effects and Other Self-Fulfilling Prophecies in Organizations." *Leadership Quarterly*, Winter 1992, pp. 271–305.
11. Epley, N., and Dunning D. "Feeling 'Holier Than Thou': Are Self-Serving Assessments Produced by Errors in Self- or Social Prediction?" *Journal of Personality and Social Psychology*, Dec. 2000, pp. 861–875.
12. Schulz, K. *Being Wrong: Adventures in the Margin of Error*. London: Portobello Books, 2010.
13. Brafman, O., and Brafman, R. *Sway: The Irresistible Pull of Irrational Behavior*. New York: Doubleday, 2008.
14. Miller, A. G., and Lawson, T. "The Effect of an Informational Option on the Fundamental Attribution Error." *Personality and Social Psychology Bulletin*, Jan. 1989, *15*(2), 194–204.
15. Schulz, *Being Wrong*.
16. Keegan, R. *In over Our Heads: The Mental Demands of Modern Life*. Cambridge, MA: Harvard University Press, 1994.

Chapter 3

1. Barsade, S. "The Ripple Effect: Emotional Contagion and Its Influence on Group Behavior." *Administrative Science Quarterly*, Dec. 2002, pp. 644–675.
2. Lord, R. G., Brown, D. J., and Freiberg, S. J. "Understanding the Dynamics of Leadership: The Role of Follower Self-Concepts in the Leader/Follower Relationship." *Organizational Behavior and Human Decision Processes*, June 1999, 78(3), 167–203.

Chapter 4

1. Senge, P. "The Leader's New Work: Building Learning Organizations." *Sloan Management Review*, Fall 1990. http://sloanreview.mit.edu/article/the-leaders-new-work-building-learning-organizations/.
2. Beinhocker, E. "The Adaptable Corporation." *McKinsey Quarterly*, 2006, *2*, 77–87.
3. Magretta, J. "The Power of Virtual Integration: An Interview with Dell Computer's Michael Dell." *Harvard Business Review*, Mar. 1998, pp. 72–84.
4. Starkey, K., and Hall, C. "The Spirit of Leadership: New Directions in Leadership." In S. A. Snook, N. Nohria, and R. Khurana (eds.), *The Handbook for Teaching Leadership: Knowing, Doing, and Being.* London: SAGE, 2011.
5. Cooper, R., and Sawaf, A. *Executive EQ: Emotional Intelligence in Leadership and Organizations*. New York: Berkeley Publishing Group, 1997.
6. Roberto, M. "Lessons from Everest: The Interaction of Cognitive Bias, Psychological Safety and System Complexity." *California Management Review*, 2002, *45*, 136–158.
7. Costa, P., and McCrae, R. "Four Ways Five Factors Are Basic." *Personality and Individual Differences*, June 1992, pp. 653–665.
8. Argyris, C., and Schön, D. *Organizational Learning: A Theory of Action Perspective*. Reading, MA: Addison-Wesley, 1978.
9. Rogers, C. *On Becoming a Person: A Therapist's View of Psychotherapy*. London: Robinson, 1995. (Originally published 1961.)

Chapter 5

1. Bar-On, R. *EQ-i Technical Manual*. Toronto: MHS, 2004.
2. Newman, M. *Emotional Capitalists*. Sydney: RocheMartin, 2005.

3. Salovey, P., and Caruso, D. *The Emotionally Intelligent Manager*. San Francisco: Jossey-Bass, 2004.

Chapter 6

1. Kahneman, D. *Thinking, Fast and Slow*. New York: Penguin Books, 2011.
2. Evans, H. J. *Winning with Accountability*. Dallas, TX: CornerStone Leadership Institute, 2008.

Conclusion

1. Greitens, E. *The Heart and the Fist: The Education of a Humanitarian, the Making of a Navy Seal*. New York: Mariner, 2012.
2. Chatman, J., and Kennedy, J. "Psychological Perspectives on Leadership." In N. Nohria and R. Khurana (eds.), *Leadership: Advancing the Discipline*. Boston: Harvard Business School Publishing, 2010.
3. Fletcher, J. K. "The Paradox of Post Heroic Leadership: An Essay on Gender, Power and Transformational Change." *Leadership Quarterly*, 2004, *15*(5), 647–661.
4. Quoted in Nye, J. *Soft Power: The Means to Success in World Politics*. New York: Public Affairs, 2004.
5. Kayes, D. C. *Destructive Goal Pursuit: The Mt. Everest Disaster*. New York: Palgrave-Macmillan, 2006.
6. LeDoux, J. E. *Synaptic Self: How Our Brains Become Who We Are*. New York: Viking, 2002.
7. Csikszentmihalyi, M. *Flow: The Classic Work on How to Achieve Happiness*. London: Rider, 2002.
8. Meikle, A. "High Performance Leadership." In S. A. Snook, N. Nohria, and R. Khurana (eds.), *The Handbook for Teaching Leadership: Knowing, Doing, and Being*. London: SAGE, 2011.
9. "Stanley McChrystal: Listen, Learn . . . Then Lead." TED Talks. Filmed Mar. 2011, posted Apr. 2011. http://www.ted.com/talks/stanley_mcchrystal.html.
10. Kramer, R. M. "The Harder They Fall." *Harvard Business Review*, Oct. 2002, 58–66.

Acknowledgments

We both thank all of those people with whom we have worked through the years and from whom we learned so much, especially those clients who provided us with the stories we have used in this book. A special thanks to our senior editor, Karen Murphy; our developmental editor, Christine Moore; our agent, Cynthia Zigmund; and the fantastic team of experts at Wiley who helped us collect and edit our thoughts into something readable.

Colm thanks Pat Given, who remains his model of an ideal leader. Also his parents, who instilled in him from an early age a respect for learning and education, and his wonderful children, Emma, Ian, Megan, Nessa, and Ciara. They have made him want to be the best dad he can be. He apologizes for all the times when you had to be quiet 'cause Dad was working on that darn book! And, last, to Breda, friend, soul mate, partner, love of his life . . . thank you.

Henry thanks his parents for modeling unconditional love, his grandparents for emigrating to the United States, and Ana Lucia for editing his work and tolerating him during the writing process. Also to his circle of friends and family, who provide challenge and support every day, specifically Bruce Malott, David Plummer, Bob Irish, and Michael Tinsley for having faith in him when he stumbled, and who supported him as he dusted himself off. Thanks also to his first publisher, David Cottrell, and to his team at Dynamic Results, namely, his advisory board, Wendy Beecham, Adam Salacuse, and Jerry Hoag; the amazing team of consultants at Dynamic Results, who perform miracles for our clients; and the Dynamic Results internal operations team, including Debra Padilla and Ede Ericson Cardell.

About the Authors

Henry Evans is founder and managing partner of Dynamic Results, LLC, providing consulting and coaching solutions to such companies as Samsung, Toyota, 3M, adidas, New York Life, and Allstate. He has logged over ten thousand hours of coaching executives and leaders, offering behavioral assessment and development along with helping them tackle challenges in tactical, strategic, and relational matters and write and implement their business strategies. He is the author of *Winning with Accountability: The Secret Language of High-Performing Organizations*.

Henry is also a former chairman of Vistage, the world's largest organization of CEOs, and was president and CEO of various national companies, which he owned and founded. These companies were members of the Advantage Group, which he also owned and founded. Prior to forming the Advantage Group, Henry worked as an independent business consultant focusing on quality control initiatives.

Henry lectured on business ethics at the Anderson School of Management and earned the Business Leadership Center's Teaching Excellence Award at the SMU Cox School of Business fourteen times. He also is qualified as an assessor of emotional intelligence, is a facilitator in strategic planning certified by the

Institute of Cultural Affairs, and is certified as a master assessor in using the Retention Edge leadership assessment tool.

Born and raised in New York City, Henry currently resides in San Francisco.

Colm Foster, PhD, senior associate of Dynamic Results, specializes in working with executives and their teams to improve individual and team effectiveness. His clients have included adidas, Danske Bank, Kerry Group, Bacardi, Thompson Reuters, Irish Life, GlaxoSmithKline, Irish Stock Exchange, and Bank of Ireland. He qualified as a chartered accountant with Ernst and Young in Dublin and spent a number of years with Price-Waterhouse in Australia. He was finance director, strategy director, and customer service director for the Irish subsidiary of Diageo.

Since 2005, Colm has worked as a performance coach to senior executives in Europe, Asia, and the United States, providing consultation in talent development, strategy development and execution, high-performance team work, and leadership development. Colm's leadership research has involved working with the U.S. Marines, the Royal Marine Commandos, and the Jesuit Order. Colm is a fellow of the Institute of Chartered Accountants in Ireland. He holds an MBA from University College Dublin, an MA in organizational behavior from Dublin City University, and a PhD in leadership and emotional intelligence from University College Dublin. He is a member of the adjunct faculty of the Michael Smurfit Graduate Business School, the Irish Management Institute, and Dublin City University.

For more information, please visit www.dynamicresults.com.

Index

Page references followed by *fig* indicate an illustrated figure; followed by *t* indicate a table.

Q

R

S

MEET THE AUTHORS

Henry Evans is Change Excellence Officer (CEO) and Founding Partner for Dynamic Results, specializing in strategy execution, executive development, and emotionally intelligent leadership. His first book, *Winning WIth Accountability*, was published in 2008. He lives in San Francisco, CA, USA.

Colm Foster specializes in working with executives and their teams to improve individual and team effectiveness. He is an adjunct faculty member of University College Dublin and holds a PhD and MBA. Colm lives in Dublin, Ireland with his family.

For more information, please visit
www.dynamicresults.com

Made in the USA
Middletown, DE
30 May 2023